HOW TO COMBAT DECISION FATIGUE

HOW TO CLEAR YOUR MIND FROM OVERWHELM, DODGE PROCRASTINATION PITFALLS, AND RISE WITH CLEARER AND WISER DECISIONS

WISDOM UNIVERSITY

CONTENTS

Exclusive Offer

4 Bonuses + Free Access To ALL Our Upcoming Books!

Free Bonus #1

Our Bestseller
How To Train Your Thinking
Total Value: $9.99

If you're ready to take maximum control of your finances and career, then keep reading...

Here's just a fraction of what you'll discover inside:

- Why hard work has almost nothing to do with making money, and what the real secret to wealth is
- Why feeling like a failure is a great place to start your success story
- The way to gain world-beating levels of focus, even if you normally struggle to concentrate

"This book provides a wealth of information on how to improve your thinking and your life. It is difficult to summarize the information provided. When I tried, I found I was just listing the information provided on the contents page. To obtain the value provided in the book, you must not only read and understand the provided information, you must apply it to your life."

NealWC - Reviewed in the United States on July 16, 2023

"This is an inspirational read, a bit too brainy for me as I enjoy more fluid & inspirational reads. However, the author lays out the power of thought in a systematic way!"

Esther Dan - Reviewed in the United States on July 13, 2023

"This book offers clear and concise methods on how to think. I like that it provides helpful methods and examples about the task of thinking. An insightful read for sharpening your mind."

Demetrius - Reviewed in the United States on July 16, 2023

"Exactly as the title says, actionable steps to guide your thinking! Clear and concise."

Deirdre Hagar Virgillo - Reviewed in the United States on July 18, 2023

"This is a book that you will reference for many years to come. Very helpful and a brain changer in you everyday life, both personally and professionally. Enjoy!"

Skelly - Reviewed in the United States on July 6, 2023

Free Bonus #2
Our Bestseller
The Art Of Game Theory
Total Value: $9.99

If Life is a game, what are the rules? And more importantly... Where are they written?

Here's just a fraction of what you'll discover inside:
- When does it pay to be a selfish player... and why you may need to go inside a prisoner's mind to find out
- How to recognize which game you're playing and turn the tables on your opponent... even if they appear to have the upper hand
- Why some games aren't worth playing and what you should do instead

"Thanks Wisdom University! This book offers simple strategies one can use to achieve things in your personal life. Anyone of average intelligence can read, understand and be in a position to enact the suggestions contained within."

David L. Jones - Reviewed in the United States on November 12, 2023

"Haven't finished it yet, but what I've gone through so far is just incredible! Another great job from this publisher!"

W. S. Jones - Reviewed in the United States on October 12, 2023

"A great book to help you through difficult and complex problems. It gets you to think differently about what you are dealing with. Highly recommend to both new and experienced problem solvers. You with think differently after reading this book."

Thom - Reviewed in the United States on October 18, 2023

"I like this book and how it simplifies complex ideas into something to use in everyday life. I am applying the concept and gaining a lot of clarity and insight."

Ola - Reviewed in the United States on October 18, 2023

"The book is an excellent introduction to game theory. The writing is clear, and the analysis is first-rate. Concrete, real-world examples of theory are presented, and both the ways in which game theory effectively models what actually happens in life is cogently evaluated. I also appreciate the attention paid to the ethical dimensions of applying game theory in many situations."

Amazon Customer - Reviewed in the United States on October 8, 2023

Free Bonus #3

Thinking Cheat Sheet
Break Your Thinking Patterns
Total Value: $4.99

Free Bonus #4

Thinking Sheet
Flex Your Wisdom Muscle
Total Value: $4.99

A glimpse into what you'll discover inside:

- How to expose the sneaky flaws in your thinking and what it takes to fix them (the included solutions are dead-simple)
- Dozens of foolproof strategies to make sound and regret-free decisions leading you to a life of certainty and fulfillment
- How to elevate your rationality to extraordinary levels (this will put you on a level with Bill Gates, Elon Musk and Warren Buffett)
- Hidden gems of wisdom to guide your thoughts and actions (gathered from the smartest minds of all time)

Bonus #5

Get ALL our upcoming books for FREE
(Yes, you've read that right)
Total Value: $199.80*

You'll get exclusive access to our books before they hit the online shelves and enjoy them for free.

Here's everything you get:

✓ How To Train Your Thinking eBook	($9.99 Value)
✓ The Art Of Game Theory eBook	($9.99 Value)
✓ Break Your Thinking Patterns Sheet	($4.99 Value)
✓ Flex Your Wisdom Muscle Sheet	($4.99 Value)
✓ All our upcoming eBooks	($199.80* Value)

Total Value: $229.76

Take me to wisdom-university.net for my free bonuses!

(Or simply scan the code with your camera)

Scan Me

*If you download 20 of our books for free, this would equal a value of 199.80$

WHAT READER'S ARE SAYING ABOUT WISDOM UNIVERSITY

"I have been reading books from Wisdom University for a while now and have been impressed with the CONDENSED AND VALUABLE INFORMATION they contain. Reading these books allows me to LEARN INFORMATION QUICKLY AND EASILY, so I can put the knowledge to practice right away to improve myself and my life. I recommend it for busy people who don't have a LOT of time to read, but want to learn: Wisdom University gives you the opportunity to easily and quickly learn a lot of useful, practical information, which helps you have a better, more productive, successful, and happier life. It takes the information and wisdom of many books and distills and organizes the most useful and helpful information down into a smaller book, so you spend more time applying helpful information, rather than reading volumes of repetition and un-needed filler text.

—Dawn Campo, Degree in Human psychology and Business, Office administrator from Utah

"I came to know about Wisdom University from the Amazon Kindle. There were recommendations for some of the Wisdom University books. Found every book very interesting. I really loved it. Subscribed for the free material which was delivered right into my inbox. Since then, I have been a fan. I couldn't buy the books... since am in a situation. But as soon as I get a sufficient amount, I plan to purchase some nice titles that piqued my interest. I recommend the books to everybody who wants to live a life free from all sorts of mental blocks that reflect in real life. These books are definitely the lighthouse, especially for those crawling through the darkness of ignorance. I wish Wisdom University all the best."

—Girish Deshpande, India, 44, Master of Veterinary Science, working as an Agriculturist

"I wanted to read some books about thinking and learning which have some depth. I can say "Wisdom University" is one of the most valuable and genuine brands I have ever seen. Their books are top-notch at kindle. I have read their books on learning, thinking, etc. & they are excellent. I would especially recommend their latest book "Think Like Da Vinci" to those who want to have brilliant & clear thinking."

—*Sahil Zen, 20 years old from India, BSc student of Physics*

"I associate Wisdom University with critical thinking and knowledge improvement. It is helpful for critical thinkers and all those who are interested in improving their knowledge."

—Elliot Wilson, MBA and Doctor of Business Administration (DBA), Chief Growth Officer

"I have most of the ebooks & audiobooks that Wisdom University has created. I prefer audiobooks as found on Audible. The people comprising Wisdom University do an excellent job of providing quality personal development materials. They offer value for everyone interested in self-improvement."

—*Neal Cheney, double major in Computer-Science & Mathematics, retired 25yrs USN (Nuclear Submarines) and retired Computer Programmer*

"I've been working my way through the Wisdom University books. It's been a couple months now, and I'm enjoying exploring new ideas and new ways at looking at things. I think these books are helpful for anyone who wants to improve their thinking skills, particularly in business settings. They're also an option for people who are just generally interested in self-improvement."

—Drew Del, Hawaii (USA), 48, Post-grad cert in Education, works as Entrepreneur & Researcher

"Wisdom University embodies an innovative and progressive educational approach, expertly merging deep academic insights with contemporary learning techniques. Their books are not only insightful and captivating but also stand out for their emphasis on practical application, making them a valuable resource for both academic learning and real-world personal development."

"I'm a subscriber of Wisdom University for over a year now. I would recommend Wisdom University books to anyone who wants to improve their understanding of cognitive behavioural therapeutic principles."

INTRODUCTION

It was life or death, but it wasn't an easy choice. Nando Parrado and Roberto Canessa debated the likelihood of survival for themselves and everyone they felt responsible for if they continued to wait on the mountain for help or attempted to hike to civilization for help in their weakened state.

Almost two months prior, their plane had crashed on the side of a mountain in the Andes Range. The plane had split in two, the radio was toast, and the pilot was dead. [1] Somehow, despite seeing rescue planes searching in the area, no one had spotted them. Their initial food resources were long gone, and the surviving passengers had resorted to cannibalism to survive, but even the dead bodies were running out.

Nando and Roberto were the strongest left, although even their strength was barely there anymore. They were exhausted, discouraged, fighting absolute hopelessness, and they had to make a decision: stay or find help. Neither option guaranteed survival, and both seemed to offer an equal chance of death. It took them days to decide but they finally decided to try a new tactic and hike out. The worst that could happen was death, which they were already waiting for.

Although many people never have to face such extreme scenarios, the weight of making choices can make it feel like they are. When people are bombarded by decisions, especially those that impact others, it can easily become overwhelming. Feelings of hopelessness and confusion can set in as all potential outcomes of each decision filter through the mind. The impact on employees, on themselves, and the company they work for can feel like too much responsibility. Despite every attempt to make wise decisions, results seem to fall flat. The quality of work suffers, and dissatisfaction with what was once enjoyable and even meaningful seems to pervade. Best efforts don't seem to make any progress, and people anxiously seek solutions. Unfortunately, for many people, the only solution they can see is to work harder and longer. This is not the only solution. In fact, it isn't even a good one.

Rather than simply working harder and longer, working more efficiently, doing more with less, is a more viable solution. A person can't get to this place of efficiency without understanding why they aren't there in the first place. Knowing the root causes of being overwhelmed and stuck is the first step in finding forward momentum.

Knowledge shifts the way people think about their world and offers a wise perspective without judgment. It offers solutions, strategies, and tactics to move out of the mud and into clarity and results.

It might feel overwhelming to think about adding another task to your to-do list by reading an entire book. When there is already so much to do that nothing ever seems to get done, the value of reading a book often isn't recognized. Having lessons that take others years to learn succinctly laid out ultimately saves time and energy resources. It is much easier to learn from the experiences and mistakes of others than it is to learn them yourself. It is much less time-consuming to read the book than it is to find the sources and read them yourself.

Many people wait until they find themselves completely exhausted and unable to see a way out of their fog before taking steps to change this. By this point, they are too tired to absorb much of the information they need. I have learned my lessons slowly, over years of struggle. My progress happened in baby steps, barely making waves until I found myself on medical rest. I was exhausted, coming home each night with barely enough energy to walk the dog let alone make dinner. I was having dizzy spells at work, often catching myself on furniture to avoid passing out, and intense stomach pain that prevented me from eating. I was losing too much weight too quickly. When I went to the dentist, she sat down beside me and gently asked if I struggled with bulimia since the enamel on my teeth was disintegrating as a result of excess stomach acid. I didn't, although I couldn't blame her for asking. I knew the cause: the stress of keeping up, of always appearing productive, and of trying to be perfect at work had caught up with me physically. When I went in to see my doctor, I found myself in tears, confiding to him that I just couldn't do it anymore. I couldn't keep up with demands of work and home, and I felt incapable of handling the stress and anxiety. I also felt my confidence crumbling–I wasn't good at what I did anymore. He prescribed medication to help rebuild the lining of my stomach and seven months off work.

During that time, and in the following years, I scoured all possible resources for knowledge and strategies to avoid feeling the pressures of work and life and prioritize what was important to me: rest, family, fun, *and* success at work. I apply the knowledge I gained, and have experienced greater success with more ease and joy than ever before.

This book offers my time and knowledge to readers. In reading, one can gain understanding of the root cause of difficulty making decisions, how society is set up for a lack of productivity and success, and then how to counter these things. Practical strategies are mixed with practical and scientific knowledge to provide an understanding that frees people from the pressure they put on themselves and the pressure others put on them. By amalgamating the information from various studies and translating it into applicable scenarios and strategies, this book becomes a valuable resource. If you are truly ready to see change in your life, to change the way you work, and to put in some effort to eventually put in less, then this book won't simply sit on your shelf waiting to be picked up someday. It will offer immediate strategies with solutions to current problems.

Brittany Valenzuela

1

DEFINING DECISION FATIGUE

WHY IS IT SO DIFFICULT FOR US TO MAKE A DECISION?

M ichelle slumped onto her couch. She felt heavy, as though the weight of the world sat in her lap. It had been a long week, and she was glad it was almost over because she had no energy left for anything else. Just then, her phone beeped, notifying her of a text. She glanced at the screen and immediately remembered that she still hadn't replied to a friend's goodbye party invitation. The invite had come two weeks ago, but Michelle had so many things to think about at work with the two new employees on her team who seemed to think nothing was important. It took every ounce of energy not to yell at them. To top it off, her mom had recently decided to explore new treatment options, with Michelle as her advisor. She just didn't have the time to think about the invitation. She let out a frustrated groan. She could barely decide what to feed her grumbling stomach, let alone muster the mental capacity to talk to strangers at a party. She sighed and told herself she would reply after she ate something.

Michelle slowly pulled herself up from the couch and toward her kitchen, where she opened the fridge. Staring at the lettuce, carrots, celery, and other fresh items, she couldn't figure out what to make. Instead, she pulled a bag of chips out of the pantry and trudged back to the couch. She turned on the TV and scrolled through Netflix as she crunched the chips. An hour later, she still hadn't chosen anything to watch, the empty bag of chips lay beside her on the couch, and she was just as exhausted as when she came home. She sighed and wondered what had happened to her.

She used to be a go-getter. She had energy for everything, loved going to work in the mornings, consistently achieved outstanding results at work, went to the gym regularly, and had a social life. Now she felt as though she could barely function. Her performance at work was slipping, she found herself zoning out while her mom discussed new medications, and she hadn't been out with friends or to the gym in weeks. She felt her anger rising; she was frustrated with herself and her life. She needed to find ways to be more efficient and get more done quickly, but she didn't seem to have the energy even to try.

Michelle's phone beeped again, reminding her of the waiting message. She stared at her phone, guilt rising, before leaving it where it was and going to bed.

What Michelle feels is familiar to many people who live busy lives with many responsibilities and demands on their time and attention. Sometimes people think these feelings are the expected result of making a living. When they try to meet all the demands of work and find time for family and friends, they can get lost in the chaos and feel overwhelmed. Scrolling through social media doesn't help their case. They see people living exciting lives doing everything they wish they could, and they wonder how others manage it all. They feel guilty that they can't make it happen for themselves, and their self-confidence begins to fail. They begin to think there is something wrong with them.

There is nothing wrong with them, though. They simply have a finite capacity that is often over-taxed. You might feel the same way as you try to find time for a life outside of work that provides relaxation and rest from the demands of your job. You might be striving for more time with your family and friends or wishing your job didn't take up so much of your time and energy. You also have a limited measure of energy resources. When you begin to understand this, you can take steps to change your thinking and your life.

The Infinite Energy Fallacy

Society tells people they can do it all and have it all. People are bombarded with this message in advertisements, television shows and movies, motivational talks, literature, social media, and work environments.

Almost everywhere they look, they are encouraged to put their energy forward and strive to have it all. It feels like a positive message to get behind and ultimately find joy in. Who doesn't want to believe they are capable and strong enough to have everything they want in every area of their life? People don't realize that there is a cost to having it all in the way society expects them to go about getting it.

People's social media portrays them smiling on luxurious vacations with their family and photos of exciting activities, but these photos only show a part of the picture. The vacation picture doesn't have a hashtag revealing the grueling hours of work that might be behind the bonus paying for the trip or the relief that they finally get to spend time as a family. The pictures of exciting activities don't show the times when they wished they weren't stuck behind their desk doing a job they no longer felt passionate about. Despite the hidden reality, these posts create pressure to have it all and do it all. People feel the need to keep up a high level of activity, to outperform at work, to be socially active, to spend time with their family, and to be happy about it all. Over time, they feel themselves fading physically, mentally, and emotionally. They can't figure out how to find their way back to the person they were. They feel it should be easy because that is the constant message from the world around them: work out more often to gain more energy, put in more time at work in the short term for long-term rewards–work harder and somehow that will make everything better. The truth is that people often end up experiencing the opposite, draining themselves further instead of achieving the promised results.

Greg McKeown explains the paradox of success in his book *Essentialism: The Disciplined Pursuit of Less*. People begin with passion and purpose in their careers or at the start of a new job. They are excited to begin sharing their ideas, showcasing their skills, and contributing to something meaningful. As a result, they are successful; managers and colleagues are impressed and trust them. This reliance leads to increased responsibilities and more impressive tasks. People are justifiably proud of their accomplishments and the recognition that comes with them. Unfortunately, there is a dark side to this success. People begin to demand more, and more time and effort is spent completing the assigned tasks, slowly draining energy reserves. The result of this experience can be an inability to contribute meaningfully, leading to a lack of clarity and purpose. [1]People can become unproductive and often lose confidence in themselves and their abilities. [2] They think they are the problem. This paradox is mirrored in other areas of life as people work to create the ideal life for themselves and their families. Ultimately there is no room to rest or reevaluate goals.

The truth is that People can't do it all. And that is okay. Social and biological sciences are proving that humans, like rechargeable batteries, have a finite amount of energy, and when they use up that energy, they need to recharge.

<u>The Spoon Theory</u>

Christine Miserandino came up with a succinct and easy way to explain the idea of finite energy. Miserandino lives with Lupus, a chronic illness that can be difficult to understand. So, when her friend asked her what life was like with Lupus, Miserandino collected every spoon in sight at the diner they frequented. She then handed them to her friend and told her the spoons represented her energy resources for the day. Miserandino then told her friend to run through her day from the beginning to the end, and at each task or choice she had to make, Miserandino took away a spoon.

Her friend had to think carefully about how to spend her spoons since she only had twelve with no option to access more. At first, it seemed relatively simple: a spoon for getting ready, a spoon for the first task at work, a spoon for a meeting, etc. Twelve spoons seemed like enough. It wasn't until Miserandino broke down each task that her friend understood the severity of her limited resources.

Getting ready in the morning didn't cost a single spoon. Instead, waking up and getting out of bed was one spoon. Showering was another spoon. Making breakfast was one more spoon. Getting dressed costed a spoon. Her friend realized that by the time she was ready to go out the door to work, she had used at least four spoons, and her day ahead was long. With only eight spoons left, every choice was more difficult to make. Every decision and action needed careful thought and consideration. [3]

This activity, dubbed "The Spoon Theory," spread beyond Miserandino and her friend to the world. It provides an easy way to understand what it is like to live with a chronic illness and what it is like to think about and make many decisions in a day–a position everyone is in, no matter their health status.

Studies estimate that the average adult makes 35,000 decisions every day. [4] These decisions range from what to wear to what to do about an insubordinate employee. The Spoon Theory suggests that with each decision people make, they have smaller reserves of mental capacity for the next decision. More and more studies support this explanation and reveal the limited ability to make decisions in a day. Scientists refer to this condition as Decision Fatigue.

The Myth Dispelled

Everyone begins their day by eventually getting out of bed; this is one of many decisions people will make in a day. For most, getting out of bed feels reflexive, but there is a biological and mental process connected to this simple task.

Many people wake up and wonder if they press the snooze button on the alarm or get out of bed immediately. They think about the consequences of each choice, even in their sleepy state. If they press the button, they risk ending up in traffic and being late, or they have to decide to skip breakfast for the extra few minutes of sleep. People weigh every possibility and every hypothetical outcome, using previous experiences to help them make this first choice of the day. [5] Even if their habit is to get out of bed right away, at one time in the past, they had to think about this choice, and their brain and body remember the emotions experienced because of that decision. [6] Those emotions are the reason they continue to make the same choice repeatedly.

What feels like a simple choice is a complex process that uses up the first spoon of energy for the day. Once someone gets out of bed, thousands of choices will follow. If they don't live alone, they must make decisions surrounding interaction with others. At work, they have to decide what tasks to complete first, which meetings to attend, how much time to spend chatting with colleagues, which colleagues to spend time with, and which ones to avoid; they have to make decisions about scheduling–the list is endless. By the end of the day, they feel entirely drained; they have reached decision fatigue. By definition, they have become unable to make quality decisions or demonstrate self-control as a result of making multiple choices. [7]

Decision fatigue isn't always this obvious, and, commonly, people are unaware they are experiencing it. However, it is vital to be aware of this condition because the symptoms of decision fatigue are more harmful than mere exhaustion.

When someone has to make many decisions while being bombarded with information from multiple sources about each choice they make, they become mentally incapable of determining the wisest choice. This incapability manifests in two extreme ways: recklessness and decision paralysis.

Recklessness

People commonly relate self-control to actions like not eating a second piece of cake or not letting their emotions get the better of them. However, the ability to control one's actions is much broader than these examples. Self-control underlies each choice people make, and it can be exhausting to exercise it throughout the day.

Imagine being in a meeting that is running long. You have at least a few hours of work ahead of you before your next meeting, so you know you will have to skip lunch, and it feels like the discussion is never going to end. Just as it seems things are wrapping up, one of your colleagues asks a clarifying question you don't perceive as being particularly important. You take a deep breath, close your eyes, and clench your teeth to prevent the explosion of frustration you feel building up inside you.

This simple act of self-control is more taxing than it might seem, and after several displays of self-control in the course of a day, people lose their ability to control their emotions. [8] At this point, they begin to act recklessly because they can no longer demonstrate self-control or think clearly about the potential consequences of their actions.

Self-control and the effort it takes to make choices are inextricably linked. Moments when people must demonstrate self-control bombard them throughout the day. They might need to exercise restraint when they're hungry and craving a sugary snack. They are resisting the temptation to eat something unhealthy while also making a choice regarding what to do about their hunger: choosing a healthier option or having a cup of tea instead. Similarly, when their boss tells them the deadline for a project has been bumped up, they fight to control their frustration while also choosing how to respond: simply agreeing, fighting for more time, or agreeing with the added comment that the changed deadline isn't fair and will compromise quality of work.

Every time a person is required to demonstrate self-control, there is a complicated biological and mental process that uses their energy reserves. If someone must engage in this process many times throughout the day, they are less likely to have the energy to fight their emotions or temptations by the end of the day. As a result, actions can become impulsive and even damaging, and emotions can intensify. [9] A single glass of wine at dinner can quickly turn into an entire bottle, further inhibiting the ability to make wise decisions. [10] More acute emotions can result in rash choices that counter perceived negative emotions. For example, a sudden and intense surge of anger may result in a person saying things they wouldn't usually say to relieve them of the anger they feel. It may also result in weaving through traffic at top speed to get past a single slow driver to ease the frustration felt at being stuck behind someone who is not in as much of a hurry. With more intense emotions, it is more difficult to resist the urges that accompany them.

One of the greatest temptations people struggle to resist because of decision fatigue related to self-control is the urge to rest from work with a short television or internet break. [11] Falling prey to these temptations means less productivity. It sets us up for the loss of purpose and clarity Greg McKeown discusses in his book *Essentialism*. [12] In addition to the inability to resist temptations, decision fatigue degrades a person's ability to reason and think clearly about the outcomes of a decision. [13] So, when experiencing decision fatigue, one cannot think about the big picture, but instead tends to make a choice that satisfies their current desire. For example, if someone is faced with the option to accept or reject a team project at work, they may choose not to take on the project because they feel they cannot deal with the dynamics of a team in the next week. They may fail to realize that the project aligns with their goals and passions and, in the long run, could set them up for a promotion. The decision to reject the project is not due to the person's lack of foresight. Rather it is due to their brain's inability to cognitively think about the potential long-term benefits. In this case, decision fatigue can result in stagnancy in one's life.

Decision Paralysis

The impacts of intensified emotions, lack of self-control, and recklessness seem much more dangerous than the inability to choose. However, not choosing can be just as detrimental.

With decreased ability to reason in the face of a choice, people take the path of least resistance to avoid further loss of energy reserves.[14] Depending on the options, this could mean procrastination or picking the status quo—what they know works.

If someone is already exhausted, the last thing they want is to experience the stress of an emotional conflict or the possibility of facing a new circumstance. Since emotions are stronger when experiencing decision fatigue, it makes sense that people want to avoid the strong emotions that come with a decision that may not work out as well as they want it to. Instead, they make a choice they know will keep things as they are rather than introduce a change, even if there is the potential for that change to be beneficial. For example, when doctors must decide whether or not to schedule surgery for patients at the end of their shift, they are less likely to do so, even when an operation will solve the health problem more quickly and effectively. Instead, they may choose to have the patient remain in standard care. [15] Doctors are less likely to take the medical risk of surgery after making multiple patient care decisions during their shift. Although operations can be helpful, there are risks involved in each surgery, and these risks come with more emotional weight than simply leaving a patient in standard care.

Doctors are not the only people who fall prey to this symptom of decision fatigue. Judges have shown the same propensity to leave things as they are rather than make a decision resulting in change. Over ten months, researchers studied judges listening to parole hearings and deciding whether or not to grant parole. The number of cases each judge heard and decided on was tracked. In addition, researchers tracked the following elements of each case: the prisoners' crimes, the number of previous offenses, the establishment of a rehabilitation program, the time of day the hearing took place, and how close to the judges' break the hearing took place.

In the case of this study, denying parole to a prisoner avoided change and aligned with the status quo. It was clear through the study that rejecting a request was an easier decision to make than granting parole. Granting parole took longer as judges had to consider more factors in the case than if the prisoner remained in jail, even if only for a month longer, until the next parole hearing. Keeping the prisoner in jail involved less risk.

The study also revealed that judges were more likely to grant parole closer to the beginning of their day or immediately after a break during which they ate, replenishing their glucose stores. As time passed and the judges heard more cases, making an increasing number of decisions, the likelihood of granting parole decreased. Generally, a prisoner appearing at the beginning of a judge's session had a 65% chance of being granted parole. Those at the end of a session had closer to a 0% chance of receiving parole. These significant differences were consistent throughout the study, demonstrating that making decisions resulted in mental fatigue that reduced the quality of thought put into each hearing. The judges simply couldn't consider all the factors in the case, so they either put off the decision to the next hearing or simply chose to deny parole. [16]

These cases demonstrate how decision fatigue impacts the choices we make each day. In these cases, however, the doctors and judges are required to make a choice, so they choose the easiest option. There is little consideration of the long-term effects of these decisions on the people impacted. This is no fault of their own; it is simply the nature of having a finite amount of energy reserves to draw from.

The doctors and judges in these studies are not the only ones required to make important decisions at work. Everyone is faced with numerous choices throughout their day, and decision fatigue is familiar to everyone, whether they have a name for the feeling or not. As a result, there are some decisions people put off until a later time, feeling that they are not immediately important. In other words, people procrastinate, sometimes to the point of not making a decision at all and losing out on an opportunity entirely. It feels easier not to decide in the short term, but this can have catastrophic effects on a person's life in the long term. For example, someone may not have the energy to decide to lock into a mortgage rate or a natural gas rate, feeling they can put the decision off. In the meantime, the rate may increase, and they lose out on the lowest rate, creating more stress for themselves as they stretch their finances to cover the higher cost.

In Michelle's case, she could not decide about attending her friend's goodbye party. Instead, she failed to respond and went to bed, missing out on an important relational opportunity to connect with someone she cared about before they left for a long time. She couldn't understand why she was so tired and unable to do what she wanted. The truth is that she was experiencing the effects of decision fatigue in her life. She wasn't taking time to recover; instead, she was pushing herself harder, trying to catch up at work and home.

Action Steps

With the knowledge that decision fatigue exists and impacts the ability to live the life people want, it's time to look at how you can understand the implications for your own life. Are you feeling increasingly exhausted at the end of your day, unable to make wise decisions that align with your goals and values? Or do you find yourself unable to make choices, working yourself into a rut you can't seem to get out of at work, in your social life, and with your family? There is hope if this is the direction you find yourself heading.

Take a moment and outline three things you want to include in your day. Perhaps you want to have a work-free lunch at work, or perhaps you want to spend an hour actively playing with your children. Maybe you want to eat a healthy dinner. These three experiences will help you set concrete goals you can work toward as you begin to understand more about decision fatigue. Read on to learn the factors that increase these effects and how you can overcome them to live a more fulfilling life.

Chapter Summary

- Humans have a finite energy reserve that they use throughout the day.
- These energy reserves are exhausted by exercising self-control and making choices.
- The more decisions one makes, the harder it is for them to make the next one.
- Decision fatigue manifests in two significant ways: lack of self-control causing reckless choices and decision paralysis causing inaction.

2

THE BATTLE FOR ATTENTION

HOW EXTERNAL AND INTERNAL FORCES INFLUENCE OUR DECISIONS IN OUR EVERYDAY LIFE

Jason sat at his desk and looked at his calendar. His manager had just finished telling his team that they were moving in a new direction for a marketing campaign to help bring in more business. His job was to summarize the role of their team in a way that strategically targeted the consumer. He couldn't even begin to think about how to distill the complexity of his job into a list, let alone in a way that would be compelling for clients. He preferred to focus on the relational approach he was used to.

His calendar reminded him of his lunch appointment with a client in a couple of hours that he still had to prep for. He opened the client file to scroll through notes just as an inbox alert appeared on his screen. Jason clicked on the notification only to be subjected to a company-wide e-mail demanding the completion of a safety survey by the end of the day. That would have to wait; he had more pressing tasks to complete, not to mention the long list of things he hadn't finished the day before. Jason turned back to the client file to prep for his lunch meeting. A few minutes later, his phone chimed, letting him know he had a new Facebook message. He glanced at his phone. It was a message from a colleague complaining about the safety survey. Jason chuckled as he thought of a witty remark about how the company would use the survey results. He took a moment to type the comment and send it off. Seconds later, he received a like. He smiled and continued reading the client file. Over the next thirty minutes, his phone continued to chime as more people liked his comment, each time distracting him from his task. He now only had an hour to prep for his lunch meeting, and he hadn't even made it through the client file. He skimmed the rest, hoping to catch all the important notes about client preferences, and he began to devise a plan for the discussion.

After more likes to his post, ten group messages about drinks after work on Friday night, and two news alerts about the current hurricane on the east coast, Jason felt more than a little overwhelmed and behind. He was due at lunch in ten minutes—just enough time to get to the restaurant. He had barely thrown together a plan for the client meeting, and his proposal was still a work in progress. He hadn't even had a chance to think about the task his manager gave him at the morning meeting, and from the messages sent his way, it sounded like the safety survey wouldn't be a quick job.

Jason began to feel hopeless about catching up. He knew that his task list would grow over the course of the afternoon, and he would likely have to stay late tonight to catch up. He sighed and told himself it was okay because he worked better under pressure. Despite his efforts to relieve his stress, Jason felt his underlying anxiety and the belief that he wasn't good enough at his job.

It is easy to get distracted when bombarded with so many external factors. Choosing which tasks to complete or which decisions to prioritize is difficult enough when one can give it their full attention. It becomes even more difficult when they have to make those choices amid constant distractions from external stimuli or internal pressure. Decision fatigue happens faster when people constantly make choices about checking their phone, social media, e-mail, or news alerts. In a fatigued state, people can begin to doubt their abilities and no longer have the energy reserves to make the best possible decisions. [1] They start looking for instant gratification that will make them feel better through shortcuts, treats, or anything that will counter the hopelessness they feel at being overwhelmed.

External Distractions

People are used to the distractions in their lives because they surround them and have become a regular part of their environment. People often don't even realize they are being distracted. Checking their phones is second nature. They expect to hear notification after notification, and multitasking is the norm. These things work behind the scenes to reduce productivity and distract one's focus. Awakening awareness of these distractions is the first step to counteracting them.

Technology: The Dark Side Of Necessary Tools

Though opinions in the world are polarized, the truth is that most things have pros and cons depending on how people use them. The world of technology is no exception. In some ways, people's jobs and lives are easier because of social media, smartphones, portable computers, and other technology. In other ways, they become more difficult.

The use of social media and the internet is necessary for many jobs, and people often feel its use at work strengthens their bonds with colleagues, building trust they wouldn't otherwise have. [2] Social media and e-mail allow for the quick and easy exchange of information, ideas, and resources, helping to propel people's careers forward. [3] However, social interaction via social media can be a dangerous distraction, ultimately harming productivity and negatively impacting how people feel about their jobs.

As seen with Jason's story, even the notifications for social media, phone messages, and e-mail require attention. Even if someone thinks they can glance at a message, return to work, and read it later, the self-control it takes to focus when they know a message is waiting drains those finite energy resources. In addition, a decision is made with every distraction: to focus or to be distracted. After this, every other choice made is progressively more difficult. Deciding which tasks to prioritize or if an incoming request should be accepted feels overwhelming. It isn't only the self-control exerted in these scenarios that make them challenging, but the psychological processes involved.

The Marshmallow Test

Walter Mischel became famous for studying self-control and instant versus delayed gratification using marshmallows as incentives. The test was simple; he put a marshmallow in front of a child and told them they could eat it immediately or wait 15 minutes and receive a second marshmallow. The researchers then left the children alone with the treat for 15 minutes. Results varied, but most children ate the marshmallow before the 15 minutes were up. The few who didn't were given a second marshmallow. [4] Mischel continued to follow the test children as they aged and discovered that those who could wait the full 15 minutes were generally more successful in life. [5] When taken out of context, this study's results seem to justify weaknesses when it comes to caving to the temptation of checking social media or messages when one should be doing something else–instant gratification feels like it is a natural response. If people are genetically inclined to need it, there is nothing anyone can do. This belief perpetuates hopelessness and provides little motivation to change habits or thinking. When fully considering the experiment's context, the results offer less justification and more accountability for one's actions.

Prior to the marshmallow test, Mischel and his team tested the same children with other rewards. Groups of children were given a toy and told that they would receive a better one in 15 minutes. One group received the promised upgrade, establishing trust and providing motivation to wait. The other group of children never received the promised upgrade, instilling the belief that they might not get what they wanted and needed to make do with what they had. The children with established trust were far more successful at waiting for the second marshmallow because they expected it as their other toy upgrades had come. [6]

The experiment extended beyond this simple test. Mischel gave children who could not wait for a second marshmallow strategies to help them resist the temptation of instant gratification. Mischel explained the method of "cooling," the process of distancing from the things that pull a person away from their focus. This can be done in two ways: pretending and reframing.

A person can pretend the object of temptation is something different than it is. For example, they might pretend the object is not an actual marshmallow, but a toy in the shape of a marshmallow. This works because one cannot eat a toy. Others have pretended the object is merely a photo, or that it is something they do not like.

Reframing means to change the way one perceives a temptation. Mischel did this to quit smoking; he used the image of a patient with lung cancer prepped for radiation treatments to replace his thoughts about smoking. Every time he had a craving, he brought up the image of the dying patient. He broke his habit by reframing the craving to smoke into something he found unappealing. [7]

With the implementation of these strategies, the results of the test changed. Some of the children who were previously not able to withstand the temptation to eat the single marshmallow in the first test were able to wait the full 15 minutes for the second one. These children could also delay their gratification in subsequent tests. [8] It was the use of these strategies later in life that helped them become successful.

This context is essential because it shows that a person can apply strategies to delay gratification, ultimately becoming more focused, productive, and successful. When one can use techniques to minimize distractions, they can be more productive and spend their time more wisely.

Environmental Distractions

Social media and technology used within the office is only one aspect of the external distractions faced each day. The physical environment plays a crucial role in the ability to focus, efficiency, productivity, and mental health.

Scientists have found that a disorganized space causes people to produce cortisol, the hormone prevalent during stressful times. [9] Cortisol is the same hormone released when people experience the typical fight, flight, or freeze response to scenarios in which they feel threatened. Simply being in a cluttered environment begins to drain a person's energy resources as their body responds biologically, fighting the desire to focus on the surroundings instead of their job. This fight, flight, or freeze response in the context of a messy office is not a life or death situation, like being robbed at gunpoint, but the biological response is the same. The body releases the same hormone at lower levels. People don't feel the same intensity of physical reaction, so fighting might manifest in the desire to tidy or even to prioritize which areas need to be cleaned first (the tidying may never happen), effectively taking attention away from the task one needs to complete for work. If a person can exercise the necessary self-control to maintain greater focus in a cluttered environment, they deplete their energy resources more quickly. Decision fatigue sets in earlier in the day, resulting in a lack of productivity, exhaustion, and even impulsive decision-making.

There is a phenomenon called "habituation," where people become visually blind to the mess around them. In this case, they may not respond to their cluttered surroundings with the desire to clean, but they still feel the impacts physically and mentally. Even though they may not be conscious of the environmental jumble surrounding them, their brains still subconsciously respond to it. They are aware of the level of light. They smell the dust or stale air, feel the discomfort of being too hot or too cold, and hear the buzz of electronics, fans on their computers, and the consistent notifications on their phones. Each of these senses adds to the stimuli they process, increasing their heart rate and signaling their bodies to release cortisol. Cortisol doesn't just impact stress levels; when people experience prolonged exposure, it also affects their moods and cognitive abilities.

Messy atmospheres have a corresponding relationship with depression, control of mental processes, "procrastination, reduced productivity, and emotional exhaustion." [10] In addition, those who live in clutter are more prone to poorer food choices, like high-sugar snacks. As with decision fatigue, the brain craves glucose to replenish the energy lost through these biological and mental processes. Coupled with increased snacking, people who live in clutter have a higher chance of acting impulsively rather than with thought. This relationship makes sense in light of the self-control it takes to focus within clutter and the exhaustion of biological resources that happens when someone is in a messy space. These effects related to clutter are similar to the symptoms of decision fatigue. Without regulators and strategies to help in these scenarios, people set themselves up for lack of success by consistently tapping into their limited cognitive resources, diminishing their stores more quickly.

Internal Distractions

Whether it is the excessive external distractions that are the cause of struggles with mental health or whether they are a result of a preexisting condition, they can severely impact a person's ability to function and progress at work. And they play a role in the rate at which people experience decision fatigue, leading to further impairment of success.

Mental health and productivity are intrinsically linked with procrastination and perfectionism. [11] Often people with mental health conditions have a tendency to procrastinate and feel pressure to produce perfection in the work they complete. The relationship between mental health and perfectionism will be explained later as tendencies to procrastinate without the need to produce perfect results provide introduction to this correlation.

Those who suffer from a depressive state can often struggle to find the energy and motivation to complete their work or even to begin. Eventually, this can result in feelings of insecurity as there is little to no experience in celebrating productivity and success. They begin to doubt their competence, and rather than feeling this overwhelming negative feeling, they put off the task at hand for more immediate gratification.

Similarly, people with attention-deficit/hyperactivity disorder (ADHD) have difficulty focusing on a single task. The external stimuli result in constant distraction that enhances the internal thought spirals or rabbit trails that lead them almost anywhere except the task. [12] Experiencing these distractions is dismaying and can once again lead to self-doubt. Additionally, time management pressures create more stress and anxiety for these individuals, and putting the task off becomes the most gratifying option. [13] People diagnosed with obsessive-compulsive disorder (OCD) also have a penchant for procrastination. Generally, people with OCD want each decision to be the right one, wondering about every potential outcome of each decision. Sometimes, instead of making a defined choice, they will put off making a decision altogether. [14] When this relates to a work project, it becomes problematic as the task is either never completed or put off until it is too late to finish to the standard of perfection their OCD demands due to fear of making mistakes and people's expectations. [15] These pressures can often be overwhelming and lead to incomplete work and lower success rates.

[16] These difficulties are significant because they interfere with success in meaningful work, which is deemed a fundamental need for self-realization. [17] Self-realization is the final stage of Abraham Maslow's Hierarchy of Needs, during which humans find purpose, reaching the best version of themselves as contributing members of society. Therefore, it is important to understand the relationship between procrastination and mental health: procrastination and mental health go hand in hand. Whether procrastination can lead to mental health issues is yet to be proven, but it is known that people diagnosed with mental health issues tend to put things off as a result of the symptoms they experience. Without this understanding, people fall into danger of not achieving their full potential in their careers and their lives.

The Dangers Of Procrastination

Putting things off until a later can be one of the biggest temptations someone faces in a day, and most people struggle with it at some point in their lives. Of all issues related to career struggles, procrastination makes up twenty percent. Procrastination is part of human nature. The Marshmallow test proves that people consistently seek immediate pleasure first rather than delayed gratification, especially if the reward in the future doesn't hold enough value for them to perceive waiting as worthwhile. [18] Procrastinating a task one isn't particularly interested in is a form of immediate gratification.

Imagine being part of a project that does not align with your passion or career goals. Every distraction you face will make completing tasks associated with that project more challenging because you will not see completing them as worthwhile. Something like lunch with future clients, meetings for other projects, answering questions about other projects, or even completing a necessary Human Resources survey will all offer the perfect opportunity to procrastinate.

When someone completes other necessary tasks while putting off another single necessary task, it is called "active procrastination." [19] Active procrastination also includes purposefully putting off a job because the pressure of a close deadline boosts motivation and productivity. [20] This type of procrastination is common and often isn't a problem if the initial thing being postponed is eventually completed. [21] Active procrastination might even be beneficial sometimes, as people are productive and efficient at completing other tasks. Problems may arise, however, if they move into passive procrastination. [22] Passive procrastination occurs when people put off a task because they struggle to focus on it or make decisions about it, including how to start. [23] Passive procrastination also includes putting something off to experience a moment of instant gratification, also known as "the present bias." [24] In this case, people are more motivated by what they can do in the present moment rather than the rewards that will come from the completed work. This instant gratification may manifest as having a snack, spending time overviewing the likes someone gets on social media, or even the fact that the job doesn't have to be completed at that moment. Whatever someone does in these situations is not productive and results in neglecting the initial task. People end up never completing it, or they do not leave themselves enough time to produce the quality of work they need to. This situation is especially problematic if someone suffers from perfectionism.

Perfectionism

When a perfectionist procrastinates, the challenge of completing a project or task is compounded. Often, perfectionism is seen as a strength because, ideally, it produces exceptional work. [25] Perfectionism as a strength isn't a complete misconception; those striving for perfection in their jobs are also attentive to their work environment and the job requirements. As a result, they often do not suffer from procrastination as they are motivated to exceed the expectations of others and be a contributing member of their team. [26] Perfectionism correlates with procrastination and lack of productivity when worry paralyzes people from making progress. People can begin to worry too much about meeting the high standards set for them, either by themselves or others.

When someone has a high degree of concern that they cannot meet the high standards set, they will often experience anxiety and even low self-esteem. [27], [28] These impacts aren't limited to a single task or project at work, either. They often spill into other areas of their lives. They can begin to worry about whether their leadership style is perfected or even if they are qualified to do their jobs. If they voice these concerns, they are afraid others will know they cannot meet the standard, so they remain silent, unwilling to reveal their self-consciousness. Instead of talking to someone and finding reassurance or getting a reality check, they tell themselves to organize their time better, create lists, develop work rules for themselves and others, and work hard at prioritizing tasks. [29] Of course, all of these actions prevent them from pursuing the job at hand, ultimately making them active procrastinators and perpetuating the anxiety and hopelessness they feel about meeting the imagined standards they have for themselves.

Feeling as though they can't meet the imagined standards can eventually result in a deep discontent with life, morphing into other mental health concerns that ultimately lead to passive procrastination. There won't be a reason to try if someone can't meet the expectations anyway. Apathy sets in, and the ability to strive for perfection in completed work fades, leaving people floundering to achieve anything worthwhile.

Ultimately, perfectionists justify their condition with two beliefs: it protects them from results they perceive to be insufferable, and it leads to approval from others, stimulating self-esteem. [30] In its ideal form, perfectionism drives success. Unfortunately, in many cases, it does the opposite, causing people to be ineffective in their jobs and less productive as they focus unnecessary attention on tasks that likely already meet acceptable standards. Understanding the cause of perfectionism in one's life is the first step to tackling procrastination stemming from perfectionism. The next step is getting help to change one's perspective on what is realistically attainable. This change is a difficult process, and psychotherapy can be a helpful tool in this process, whether someone is diagnosed with one of the mental health issues mentioned or not. Working with a psycho-therapist can provide individuals with strategies that work specifically for a person's needs.

These strategies can help identify the reasons one cannot focus, and understanding the biological processes behind the need to procrastinate can help people move past the areas they feel stuck in their careers and their lives.

Biological Challenges

The previous section explores how a person's biological makeup can impact their ability to deal with internal and external distractions; however, the distractions also have a powerful biological impact, no matter someone's genetics. If people aren't aware of the processes happening in their brains during moments of distraction, procrastination, or perfectionist anxiety, they can't break the cycle of procrastination, mental health difficulties, hopelessness, and exhaustion. By the time they get to this cycle, their brains aren't functioning optimally, and their body's processes have become an enemy to their success. Simply put, their dopamine levels are out of balance.

Dopamine is a hormone essential in the experience of joy, positive feelings, and the promotion of a sense of general well-being. Dopamine is also vital in brain processes like thinking, making choices, focusing, motivation, sleeping, and mood. [31] People cannot complete their jobs or live their lives without each of these functions, and when dopamine levels are out of balance, each function becomes more difficult.

Understanding how dopamine levels fluctuate is key to understanding why they are essential to maintaining focus and accomplishing success. When someone makes a choice that they feel ends with a reward, their dopamine levels increase. This hormonal experience impacts the next decision they make, particularly in a comparable situation. [32] Similarly, people make decisions they know will avoid loss or punishment and, consequently, a dip in dopamine levels. [33]

Feelings of reward and punishment don't have to fall into the traditional definitions. For example, if someone decides to procrastinate on a task they are not looking forward to, their immediate reward is a feeling of pleasure and joy that they do not have to complete the task at that moment in time. As a result of this feeling, the brain releases dopamine. [34] That dopamine release begins to condition people to make a similar decision the next time they face a task they are not looking forward to, especially if there are no immediate negative consequences. [35] In this way, patterns are created that are difficult to break because the brain begins to look for a release of dopamine. [36]

On the other end of the spectrum, the punishment might be a person's disappointment in themselves for not accomplishing a task to the best of their ability. The disappointment would result in a dip in dopamine levels. Instead of feeling the joy that comes with the release of dopamine at their potential success, they feel misery and a lack of confidence in the possibility of not meeting expectations. They will intrinsically want to avoid this feeling, often resulting in the choice to procrastinate. [37] If one has never suffered a severe consequence, just the thought of procrastinating an unpleasant task will flood them with the dopamine they crave, making it more challenging to relay self-control and delay gratification. It is particularly important to consider this when one suffers from exhaustion, anxiety, depression, or perfectionism.

Feeling tired and doubting oneself are indicators of lower dopamine levels. They are unpleasant feelings that most people try to avoid however they can. At work, this may take the form of external distractions. Social media, even if viewed as an occupational tool, is a source of dopamine release. Even an indication of a message on one's phone or social media can cause a release of dopamine because these notifications are often related to positive experiences. [38] In addition, likes, emojis, and comments on the things people post excite them and positively reinforce self-worth [39]. When people feel valued that someone has made the effort to respond to them or send them a text message, their brains release dopamine. Studies have shown that this release of dopamine is similar to what happens when people addicted to drugs or alcohol satisfy their cravings. [40] This is not insignificant; rather, this is a powerful process that is difficult to fight. So when someone's phone notifies them of a message, these biological processes distract them from the task at hand, if only for a moment or two [41]. Although feeling the effects of dopamine being released feels like a relief in the moment, ultimately the procrastination method chosen ends with further stress and anxiety as people struggle to catch up after too much time spent in distraction.

In an atmosphere where someone feels frustrated, hopeless, or overwhelmed, the release of dopamine becomes more vital than ever. And when experiencing those emotions, a moment of distraction that will inevitably release dopamine and counter those negative emotions can completely derail someone, put them into procrastination mode, and send them spiraling into the world of social media. If one can resist the temptation to check their phone, that exercise in self-control drains their limited energy resources, increasing their likelihood of experiencing decision fatigue.

Every choice made includes a complex thought process connected to experiences, emotions, and perceived rewards because of an increase or decrease in dopamine levels. When someone must make several decisions a day, every one of them a multifaceted process that considers possible outcomes of risk and reward, it is no wonder they can reach decision fatigue. If someone, like Jason, begins their day with minor choices about e-mail, social media, and prioritizing tasks, they start using their energy reserves before making more significant choices. They may start the day struggling to display self-control in minor issues that arise from these activities. As a result, decision fatigue and the mental wellness challenges connected to it set in more quickly. The day will become more difficult as it drags on and stress will rise. The roller coaster of emotions that fluctuating dopamine levels straps people into adds to the exhaustion, and it is easy to find oneself overwhelmed and sometimes unable to decide.

Action Steps

Learning about the biological processes that make avoiding distraction more difficult and applying knowledge of limited decision-making capacity can help identify habits that need to be changed for the best chance at success.

To help with the identification of your personal habits, the following steps can be helpful.

1. Identify the goals you have at work that you are not meeting and think about why you might not be meeting them.
2. Write down each goal and beneath it, write down the things you are doing when you would ideally be completing the work associated with those goals.
3. Assess how much of that time is purely distraction (social media or even staring out the window ruminating on personal issues) and how much is procrastination.
4. Next, ask yourself why you perceive the immediate reward of distraction to be greater than the delayed reward of a job completed successfully.
5. The last question to ask is if there is a way to increase the perceived reward of completing the work that is being put off via distraction.

Like Jason, everyone finds themselves bombarded with distractions throughout the day that take away the ability to complete the tasks that matter to them. They begin to feel hopeless because they cannot achieve their goals, overwhelmed by their lack of time and the pressures they place on themselves to meet expectations of perfection. They leave little room to make mistakes and learn from them. The irony is that people often run out of time to perform to the best of their ability, leading to a cycle of despair and sometimes even apathy. Your story doesn't have to follow this plotline; there are some straightforward tactics that will be discussed in the coming chapters to change the trajectory of your workday, career, and life.

Chapter Summary

- Although social media and the internet can be valuable tools in most jobs, they can also cause distraction leading to a lack of productivity and eventually to the habit of procrastination.
- People with mental health issues are not the only ones who struggle with procrastination and perfectionism, but pre-existing conditions can amplify these difficulties.
- Perfectionist strivings are different than perfectionist pressures, which can be damaging and prevent productivity.
- Dopamine plays a vital role in approaching and resisting distractions at work.

3

THE MYTH OF MULTITASKING

WHY PRODUCTIVITY AS WE KNOW IT DOESN'T WORK

E fficient, versatile, productive, motivated, ambitious, reliable, focused, flexible, committed, team player, and adept are all words recommended for resume use. Employers are looking for these qualities in employees. They are also words people usually want to hear their colleagues use when they describe them. Humans take pride in their accomplishments and want others to value their contributions and, consequently, them. The compliments feel wonderful, and dopamine levels skyrocket as people bask in the glow of accomplishment. This is what has defined success. But what if all of that work is actually leading to a complete lack of productivity?

It often feels like achieving these accomplishments requires endless hours of work, sacrificing a work-life balance to be labeled with any one of those sought-after adjectives. And when someone is given these compliments, the euphoria of the dopamine release doesn't last forever; when one no longer feels the effects of the compliment, they are left exhausted and downtrodden as they face the next uphill climb in their workday.

People tell themselves this is how it must be; they justify the sacrifice with their paychecks and the adjectives people label them with. It is easy to believe there is no choice because people are surrounded by multiple sources confirming that false notion.

The Hustle

The word hustle is a complex word that has both positive and negative connotations. Someone might be "hustling" if they are cheating someone out of money, or they might be "hustling" if they are working hard to honestly acquire money. [1] This second connotative meaning conveys an attitude of admiration that permeates society. This admiration for hard work is not negative in nature; however, its manifestation within the culture can be. There is the overarching belief that people can't get anywhere if they don't work harder than others do; it is the lynchpin of success. Of course, people want to be successful, and in being so, they don't want to be called lazy or incompetent, so they do whatever they are asked to climb the ladder in their jobs, working long hours, on weekends, and sometimes even on holidays. The denotative definition of "hustle" shifts this perspective, however, and it is worth considering in relation to these expectations in attaining success.

In the context of working hard, the Meriam-Webster Dictionary defines the word hustle as "to push roughly… to convey forcibly or hurriedly…to urge forward precipitately," and "to obtain by energetic activity." [2] Rather than being something admirable, to hustle is to be rushed into things someone may not be ready for. And they are expected to do these things with energy, enthusiasm, and speed that results in a lack of care and thought. [3] Despite these negative associations with working hard and fast as society expects people to, doing so earns people respect and medals of productivity at work. People that work like this become dependable as others rely on them to get things done, finish tasks, come up with solutions to problems, and make decisions that propel the organization forward. These pressures are enormous, and they do not lessen as plates are filled with more and more tasks and projects piled atop the already full plate.

Often, details end up slipping through the cracks and the carelessness manifests, even if not intentionally. The small, everyday tasks people must complete that don't seem to directly affect their greater roles at work compound this problem. E-mails fill inboxes, waiting for answers, text messages come in with the expectation of immediate responses, and scheduled meetings take up more time than they were supposed to or need to. What initially feels like success because one is valuable enough to be given so many tasks at work begins to feel overwhelming. People find themselves floundering in these expectations and becoming less and less satisfied with the quality of their work, the meaningfulness of their roles, and the quality of their lives. They are caught in the cycle of shallow work within a culture that forces them to hastily complete many jobs to create the illusion of efficiency and productivity. [4]

Shallow Work

This illusion manifests in a to-do list that never seems to end. In fact, more often than not, it feels like it continues to grow with more tasks and projects. Electronic communications come in at an alarming rate at all hours of the day, and there is pressure in a world of mobile technology to reply almost instantaneously. Sometimes these messages are even followed up mere hours later with a request for a response. Studies have determined that, on average, employees spend 30% of their time on e-mail alone [5]. This is a staggering amount of time when many projects are unrelated to reading and responding to e-mails. When social media, reports, surveys, and other time-consuming activities that will not help us achieve our goals are added, there is hardly any time left for the work that genuinely matters to a person's job description. Yet, these tasks remain on to-do lists. In the book he wrote on focusing in a distracted work environment, *Deep Work: Rules for Focused Success in a Distracted World*, Cal Newport refers to these tasks as "shallow work." [6]

Despite the need for tools like e-mail, social media, and various online resources to complete certain aspects of many jobs, their use creates fragmented focus. The tasks related to these tools, like checking e-mail or social media responses to a campaign, do not require deep concentration or focus. These tasks do not challenge people to think innovatively about solving problems or meeting needs; they do not push people to showcase their unique skills within the context of a work project. Instead, they are easy for anyone to accomplish. In addition, people can complete these tasks amidst distractions like busy office environments, multiple notifications chiming, or even during banter between colleagues, further fragmenting their focus. People often spend the majority of their time in these jobs, attempting to complete the easy tasks first to get them out of the way and cross more items off their to-do lists, thereby creating the illusion of productivity. There are so many tasks, however, that they spend more time doing them than anything else. And because they are easy to accomplish while distracted, even more time is spent on this shallow work. People rarely give enough time to the more significant work as a result.

To dive into the ineffectiveness of shallow work, it is important to consider the definition of the word "productive." Meriam-Webster defines it as "producing, especially in abundance... yielding results, benefits, or profits." [7] The majority of the tasks many people need to complete each day, or the jobs they spend much of their time working on, do not produce an abundance of results beneficial to personal or organizational profit. These tasks do need to be completed; however, they fail to move anyone forward in their skills. Rarely does responding to e-mails, completing a safety course, or printing multiple reports for an upcoming meeting encourage skill growth or innovative thought. Shallow work only creates the illusion of productivity rather than accomplishing actual productive work.

Biological and psychological issues arise with this lack of productivity, too. By engaging in shallow work, and fragmenting their attention, people train their brains to work this way all the time. This means their attention span is reduced and distracted thinking becomes the norm. Without intervention, the ability to focus on a single thing is permanently harmed. Fragmentation also hampers one's ability to remember, wreaking more havoc on an already hectic day. There are many menial things to remember to do, and the ability to regulate emotions suffers, making everything one feels more complex and further depleting energy reserves [8]. In addition, when someone spends less time doing the things that they perceive matter to their career goals and the company's success, they can feel discouraged and disenchanted with their jobs. [9] In these cases, their productivity suffers further as they end up procrastinating, sitting at their desks wondering what happened to them and where their passion disappeared over the years [10].

Quality Of Work Life & Organizational Performance

Success is often framed by financial security resulting from a rewarding career. People usually don't imagine being stuck in a job where they receive no appreciation and find no meaning outside of a paycheck when they think about becoming successful. Instead, they imagine feeling accomplished and appreciated in a job that lacks stifling routine tasks, allows innovation, and gives them feelings of usefulness. These aspects of a job are crucial to having a good work life and, therefore, a good quality of life in general. [11] When saddled with long hours of work and an abundance of menial tasks, people have difficulty understanding how their work is meaningfully contributing to the company. They then become frustrated. People must connect most of the work they do with the corporate social responsibility initiatives of the company they work for. This awareness results in feelings of meaningful work that increases job satisfaction and lessens the emotional exhaustion faced due to shallow work. [12] Also, understanding how one's work contributes to the company's success enables a person to feel respected and valued at work; they are trusted to do important work rather than occupying their time with menial tasks that anyone else could perform. As a result, job satisfaction and quality of work life increase. [13]

In addition to understanding how one's work contributes to the company, people must also feel that they have control and autonomy over their jobs. When someone is occupied by shallow work, feeling pressured to be productive, with no time to focus on quality work or life outside of work, they become less satisfied and less productive in the end. Similarly, many companies expect so much from employees, that there is simply no way to accomplish even the meaningful tasks expected, leading to the same dissatisfaction and lack of productivity.

A study about the quality of work-life conducted in 2019 hypothesized that employees who could practice work-life balance were more likely to feel productive and that their work was meaningful and helpful to their company. [14] Interestingly, the results of their study contradicted their hypothesis and all previous research in this area. Instead of workers feeling that they were refreshed and able to do better work as a result of more time spent away from their jobs, they found that those who spent more time at work felt they were contributing to their company's success. These results were surprising because previous studies suggest that a higher ratio of time spent outside of work to time spent at work creates a sense of meaning in people's lives and their jobs. People feel they are able to perform their jobs better with greater amounts of rest, flexibility, and respect. The researchers suggest this contradiction in the data is because the company studied cultivates a culture that values longer hours of work, even if the quality of that work is lower. When employees meet these expectations, they believe they have contributed to the company's success. The researchers thought the results revealed some of the restrictive features of modern workplaces due to expectations of intense periods of work. [15]

Such a conclusion doesn't seem far-fetched when considering the pressures people often experience at work. The demand to do more in less time and to always be busy with something seems to be a symptom in most occupations and positions. Unfortunately, these standards are not sustainable, and more and more people are beginning to feel the effects of these weighty expectations. As a result, society is witnessing rising mental health issues and more cases of burnout.

Burnout

The term "burnout" is increasing in frequency as people use it to describe their exhaustion from work and life. "I'm burnt out" is a common phrase these days, and not without reason. However, burnout is more than a lack of energy and feelings of frustration and stress. When a person experiences burnout, they are impacted mentally, physically, and emotionally.

Herbert Freudenberger first used the term in the 1970s to describe his experience with burnout. His list of symptoms included "a combination of feelings, exhaustion and fatigue, a lingering cold, headache and gastrointestinal disturbances, sleeplessness and shortness of breath." [16] In the years following Freudenberger's work, the symptoms have expanded, and the definition has become more focused. Burnout is currently recognized as "severe physical and psychological stress due to the nature, type or inappropriate state of work." [17] It is apparent in the framework for studying and addressing burnout that it is a condition related solely to work stress and should not be applicable to life outside of work. The state of burnout is recognized worldwide, along with the need to create employment guidelines to protect employees from it. [18] The symptoms vary from person to person but are generally categorized into energy and emotional depletion, negativity and cynicism toward job responsibilities, and feelings of diminished competence and achievement. [19]

Symptoms such as these directly impact people's performance at work. [20] Exhaustion of energy and emotions leads to workplace errors and poor quality of work as people struggle to complete even the bare minimum of the requirements. [21] These errors are not the result of laziness or lack of effort; they are a direct result of depleted energy and emotional resources. Similarly, when social and human resource issues arise at work, there is no energy or patience to deal with them.

Negativity and cynicism can lead to the same results as employees struggle to feel hopeful about and engage with work, finding themselves more likely to procrastinate and less likely to put in the effort they used to. [22] Each task feels too big or pointless and is too difficult to complete. Eventually, feeling less competent reduces one's self-efficacy and creates doubt in abilities where there was once confidence. Depressive states and anxiety can set in, causing physical symptoms, perpetuating the cycle of procrastination, and solidifying the condition of burnout.

Identifying burnout is easy when you understand the symptoms and effects; however, when you are in it, it can be hard to recognize exactly what the cause might be. In recent decades, workloads have increased rather than decreased, resulting in greater stress and fatigue and less work-life balance. Even though burnout is a condition related solely to work, quality of life outside work and quality of life at work are intrinsically linked.

Work-Life Balance

People who have a work-life balance are more productive and often accomplish more meaningful work than those who don't. [23] The term "work-life balance" is generally understood to be an equal balance of time between one's job and personal life or the equal prioritization of one's personal and professional activities. The definition of equal time can be problematic depending on one's job and how they feel about it. The key to work-life balance is how productive a person is at their job based on the hours dedicated to it and how they feel about that time spent at work. Research shows that after 50 hours of work in a week, people's productivity per hour diminishes and after 55 hours, their productivity is so low, there is no point in working.

In many jobs, there are times when employees do need to work longer hours to ensure a project is finished on time; in these cases, hours should be calculated over the course of a month rather than strictly adhered to weekly. This means that if someone works 60 hours one week, the following week needs to ensure rest provided by fewer hours and less stressful tasks. Ensuring that work does not take up more than 50 hours a week (averaged) allows people time to engage in activities that expand the input into their brains and allows for greater productivity and creativity. Whenever someone engages in an activity, neural pathways are strengthened, developing one's skill in that specific area. As they engage in a greater number of activities, more information is absorbed, more neural pathways are formed, and the output when they engage in a work-related task is enhanced. These people are often more creative, coming up with innovations and ideas that transform rather than remain stagnant with incremental forward movement. These people move their industry or company forward. The more time spent on activities that have nothing to do with work doesn't mean less productivity at work, rather it means greater productivity and more impressive results. In the context of shallow work, creating a work-life balance ensures the production of work that is not easy to replicate by others, thereby securing one's place within their industry.

Other studies have shown that one of the key contributors to believing life at work is of poor quality is the feeling that one is working longer than they want to. [24] When longer working hours are needed to complete the tasks, there is less time and energy to do enjoyable activities outside of work that provide a diversified input for one's brain activity. In addition, people who feel they are working more than they want to can become unsatisfied with their lack of social life, lack of time spent with family, and lack of time spent exercising or on hobbies. [25] Dissatisfaction can result in feelings of cynicism and hopelessness that are key contributors to burnout.

Creating work-life balance is not always easy in a world where companies have replaced the term with phrases like "work-life integration." Rather than encouraging employees to take more time for personal priorities, this term increases the pressure to check work messages or take work calls outside of working hours since one's job is integrated with the rest of their life. [26] As a result, defining boundaries and set times for work and non-work activities is a personal responsibility. How much time is dedicated to one's job and their personal life is dependent on the individual and the responsibilities they have in each area of their life. How one is perceived at work will also impact this decision, and must be weighed against the level of productivity one feels they are able to achieve. Ultimately, this decision is not an easy one to make within the culture of most organizations, but if someone is feeling overworked, frustrated, and stressed, it is important to create these work and personal time boundaries to avoid burnout, especially in the face of any changes or periods of high stress.

Stressors & Burnout

The pandemic of 2020 brought to light many factors that can contribute to burnout. Simply moving workspaces can impact stress levels and lead to burnout. [27] Although a move in office may feel like a small change, it has many underlying factors. When people moved from working in their offices to working in their homes, the location change brought on stress. Many people shared their "office space" with children or a spouse, mimicking a change in colleagues or team changes. The nature of the tasks they completed and the demands surrounding them changed. [28] Their managers and team members were no longer accessible in person, integrating yet another stressor. [29] The entire structure of companies changed as they scrambled to reorganize, create new policies, and figure out how to continue to operate in a remote world.

These changes mimicked changes that can and do happen organizationally in the workplace. There are often changes in management, ownership, or positions within a company. Company policies change regularly to meet the ever-changing demands of clientele and employees. Spaces change, expand, and shrink as company needs change, and employees can even be moved from one office to another, or one workspace to another. Each of these changes impacts stress levels as employees shift to familiarize themselves with something new, and no matter how small a policy change or a new office location may seem, they still add to stress levels. Professors and university students who had to move their work and learn from home had higher levels of depression and anxiety related to the stress of the change. [30]

Since high levels of prolonged stress are one of the causes of burnout, these are important notes to consider to avoid burnout. If one can foresee any of these changes occurring in their job, they can mediate their stress levels with clear time boundaries to help avoid too much stress for too long. For example, someone might decide to take an extra day off in a week to help balance the time spent in a stressful environment, or they might schedule their day to include chunks of time dedicated to focusing on specific tasks to avoid the change taking up more time and energy than they need to give it. This allows people to work at their best capabilities rather than be consumed by the stress of change and risk burnout. More specific strategies are outlined in later chapters, such as methods to reduce immediate stress and ground oneself, remain calm, regulate emotions, and ultimately maintain productivity in a way that avoids burnout and decision fatigue.

Another way to avoid burnout is to do meaningful work within one's job. People must devote their time at work to tasks they perceive to be meaningful and purposeful to their company and themselves. This devotion provides a sense of agency in a job, allowing people opportunities to advance their careers in the ways they want to. This aspect of work is proven to reduce the rate of burnout in employees. [31] How does one achieve this sense of agency within their profession when they have to complete so much shallow work? Anyone can accomplish this by purposeful dedication to "deep work."

Deep Work

Deep work, unlike shallow work, cannot be accomplished while distracted because it requires intense concentration and cognitive effort; it is difficult to replicate, and as a result, reflects individual skill. Essentially, deep work is a time of "distraction-free concentration on professional activities that push our cognitive capabilities to create new value and improve skills." [32] This is not time to respond to e-mails, complete surveys, or check menial tasks off a to-do list. The results of deep work are meant to solve problems, bring something new to the table, and transform the way things are done. It is meant to give time and space for the brain to make connections between various inputs and shape that information into something meaningful for a company and ultimately for the person doing the work. Deep work takes projects to the next level and helps people grow their skills and careers. For example, deep work is not simply time taken to complete a presentation, but time to write a presentation that asks questions and challenges a person's audience in a way that propels thinking and learning and shifts perspectives as it shines light on areas no one else has thought about. Achieving these results is not an easy task; it requires mental strain, hard work, and strict boundaries.

Deep work is accomplished through time purposefully taken out of one's day to focus on a single project. Imagine a physical workspace with no phone, no television, no noise except what you choose to listen to, and no one else in the space. This space is fully and completely yours; you control who goes in, who comes out, and when. Without any distractions, the potential for complete dedication to a single task exists; the job can be completed faster since there is nothing to take away from the project at hand. There is little stress to edge its way into this time and space, preventing focus and concentration. This is the essence of deep work.

When people take the time to do deep work, they can accomplish more in less time, create new value within themselves and in projects, and improve their skills. They become invaluable as employees because they can bring new and creative solutions to their jobs with razor-sharp skills applied to the projects they tackle. They are also more likely to avoid burnout as they feel a sense of control over their work and time. [33]

Most employees begin their day by checking e-mail to see what the day holds for them. It feels like this will help them prioritize their time that day. It is a force of habit that is justified in most jobs. However, beginning the day by checking e-mail means they start draining their energy reserves early. Reorganizing the day forces people to make decisions about their schedule, prioritize tasks, and perhaps even demonstrate levels of self-control when they read an e-mail that frustrates or upsets them. Once they feel they have completed these menial tasks and can focus on their actual work, they are already suffering from decision fatigue and have jeopardized their ability to be productive in the more significant tasks.

If the day begins by setting time aside to do deep work, people can eliminate the mental fatigue that comes from making multiple small decisions and instead focus on the jobs that give meaning in the work they do. Creating the time and space for deep work is not easy and requires practice. People have become used to shallow work, and the brain must be trained to focus on a single task, to think deeply, and to concentrate on a single purpose.

Then, like with the marshmallow test, people must apply strategies to reap the maximum reward for their effort.

Not everyone has access to a space like the one described above, and even if they did, there is the issue of one's ability to focus. In a world where constant distraction is normal, multi-tasking is a sought-after skill, stress levels are high, and shallow work is the expectation; the ability to focus deeply and on a single task is rare. Brains simply aren't trained to focus on one task for an extended period of time. In fact, they are trained to look for distraction. [34] When focus is disrupted by distraction, the brain is functioning properly, as it responds powerfully to an external stimuli. [35] Speaking evolutionarily, distraction is a survival method. This means someone can't simply decide to focus deeply and suddenly find themselves doing it. The ability to focus deeply is learned, and each person needs to train their brain just as muscles are trained during a workout.

Fortunately, just as there are ways to train a muscle, there are ways to train the brain to focus deeply. Mindfulness exercises can help cognitive health, brain function, and one's ability to concentrate. These exercises help people notice what is happening in their thoughts, to observe those thoughts, and then to put them aside rather than act on them, which often increases stress. When exercising mindfulness, one's job is not to try to stop the thoughts or to judge them, but to recognize them and then refocus. It can be compared to a new client arriving early to an appointment. Each thought is a new client that should be recognized, introduced, and then should go sit on a chair in the waiting space until their designated appointment time while the current client (or focus) finishes their appointment. Although this analogy can be helpful, there are ways to make this process easier.

Training The Brain

People don't start building muscles in the gym by lifting the heaviest weights. Instead, they start with the lighter weights, slowly building their strength. When training the brain to focus, the same methodology must be followed. If someone tries to focus for hours at a time on a complex task without adequately training their brain for that mental taxation, they won't succeed. On the other hand, if someone begins with a short period of focusing on a simple task, their success will be much higher.

Mindfulness allows for shorter times of focus on simple tasks. In this way, the brain can be slowly trained for longer periods of focus. Mindfulness in its simplest form is about being present in the current moment–or being mindful of what one is experiencing in a particular moment during a specific activity. For example, a person can practice mindfulness while brushing their teeth. If they focus on the feelings and sensations of the toothbrush as they move it across their teeth and gums, the taste of the toothpaste, the feeling of the suds filling their mouth, and the saliva building, they are practicing mindfulness. Their focus on a single activity helps train the brain to focus on a single task.

Unfortunately, in real life, focusing is not this easy, and people often find their thoughts shifting from the cooling sensation of their minty toothpaste to the problem they are facing at work. When this happens, it's important to remember the analogy of a client arriving for an appointment. The thought about the problem can be recognized, introduced, and then told to wait its turn while the focus goes back to the cooling sensation of the toothpaste. This might happen by someone saying out loud or to themselves, "Ah, I do have this problem at work. It can wait. That toothpaste really does feel cold on my tongue." This mindfulness exercise can be done with any activity, offering an easy way to include mindfulness exercises into an already busy day. They are manageable ways to begin training the brain to focus on one thing at a time. As it becomes easier to focus for a short amount of time, different techniques can be used to strengthen the muscle of focus.

Short bursts of focus on a single activity are only the first step to gaining the ability to focus for longer periods of time. The next step is set a timer for a few minutes each day. If teeth brushing takes two minutes, then the timer might be set for five minutes. While waiting for the timer, sit upright with eyes closed to minimize visual distractions and breathe deeply and slowly. Focus on where the breath is felt most. This might be the lungs as they expand to take in air, or it might be the belly as it moves in and out with each breath. It may end up being both, as one feels the breath move through the body like ocean waves from the chest into the belly and then receding from the belly to the lungs and out again. Whenever thoughts, sensations, or worries surface, direct the focus back to where the breath is felt.

Practicing this simple focus helps the brain create neural pathways for concentration on a single activity. The more a person practices mindfulness exercises, the more clear the pathways become, making focus easier to achieve. [36] With more ease in this activity, the time can be increased. If one simply wants to train the brain, 12 minutes is suggested on a daily basis to help create those neural pathways and then to keep them strong. [37] Many people also engage in longer periods of mindfulness meditation for other benefits, which are discussed in later chapters.

Breathing is not the only thing a person can use to focus their attention in mindfulness exercises that will help them achieve the ability to focus. A body scan exercise is also a great way to practice focusing your attention on a single task. Body scans have the added benefit of helping a person become aware of the physical manifestations of stress, ultimately allowing them to relax and enjoy a sense of calm. To complete a body scan exercise, a person must find a comfortable position, ideally sitting or lying down. Once they are in a position that is comfortable, they focus on their toes. They can think about things like what sensations they feel in their toes (are they warm or cold?), if they are relaxed or tense, or if there is any pain or discomfort in their toes. After the toes, they can shift to their feet, then their ankles and legs, slowly moving through each body part until they reach their head. If they find their thoughts wandering away from the current body part, they can recognize the thought and gently refocus on the current body part. They may add a deep breath to the process as they go along for extra relaxation.

If there is discomfort or pain noticed in this process, it can often be corrected, preventing distraction resulting in physical pain. For example, one might notice discomfort in their toes because their shoes are tight. After a body scan, they can remove their shoes and solve that physical distraction problem. Similarly, they may notice their shoulders are tense. With this knowledge, they can take steps to relax their shoulders, preventing neck pain or a headache. They may even be able to identify what stressor is causing the tension and work to address it.

Sometimes people can mistake mindfulness exercises as a process for clearing the mind of all thoughts and therefore offering complete relaxation. This is a dangerous misconception. Unfocused attention risks the brain moving into what is called the default mode network (DMN) rather than helping to create pathways for focused attention. When the DMN is active, the mind wanders, often to major stressors. [38] The purpose of mindfulness exercises is to take control of attention and focus it on the present moment, whether that is a task for work or the sensation of the knife in the hand as someone slices carrots for dinner. [39] As one focuses on the present moment, continuously and gently reminding the brain what it needs to be thinking about whenever distracting thoughts surface, the ability to focus is improved, and it will become easier to concentrate in all areas of life. This will ultimately make deep work easier to accomplish as greater attention can more easily be directed toward the task one chooses to address in a deep work session.

How To Schedule Deep Work

The ability to accomplish deep work can move people forward in their careers and industries, and, as a result, move the companies they work for forward. Providing meaningful and purposeful work in this way helps prevent burnout by countering the lack of agency people can feel as a result of shallow work swallowing their time. But in days that are already busy, it might feel impossible to find the time to schedule time for deep work. In addition to a busy schedule, people also face external forces within their environment that might make it harder to carve out time for deep work. Taking time for deep work is counter to the work culture that is prevalent in the modern workplace, but it is not impossible. People have to set boundaries to successfully make time for deep work. These boundaries will differ for each person and will depend on the time they put aside.

Cal Newport offers four different methods of accomplishing deep work: monastic, bimodal, rhythmic, and journalistic. [40] Each of these methods offers a solution to the problem of fitting deep work into one's work life, however, not all of them are achievable for every person.

The monastic approach is the most difficult to perform as it requires extreme and total commitment to deep work. This approach requires people to schedule multiple days of deep work, sometimes for weeks on end. During this time, the focus is still on a single task, like writing a book or designing a new marketing approach or software program. The monastic method of accomplishing deep work often requires the person to be alone and removed from their daily life in a way that promotes focus. Some people have rented hotel rooms, cabins, or farms to create a space that separates them from the distractions of everyday life. [41]

Most people don't have the ability to leave their life behind for a week or more to focus on a single task. They may, however, have a day a week they can dedicate to deep work. Newport calls this method the bimodal approach. With this approach, a person can schedule a day of deep work, then move back to shallow work for a few days, and then return to a day of deep work. The deep work session is always at least one day, although if someone can manage two days at a time, they may choose to do this. [42] In this way, deep work becomes part of a regular schedule, offering the benefits of deep work without having to cloister oneself away for an extended period of time. A person may, for example, schedule every Tuesday and Thursday as deep workdays. The deep work doesn't need to last from sunrise to sunset, but takes the place of the regular workday. During this six to eight -hour day, a single task is worked on with complete focus either in an entirely different space from the rest of the week or boundaries are set that allow for no disruption from the rest of the office. No meetings should be scheduled during this time and no shallow work. [43]

The rhythmic method requires regularly scheduled times of deep work that last only a few hours at a time. [44] This is a good method of accomplishing deep work when someone is working at training their brain for focused attention. The time given to deep work isn't so long that it is exhausting to control one's thoughts and exercise self-control when it comes to resisting distractions. Spending two hours at deep work is much easier than spending 8 hours. Also, because these sessions are shorter, they can be worked into a schedule more often, becoming habit. For example, a person might come in early, stay late, or leave during the middle of the day.

- Early: arrive early at the office before anyone else comes to work, providing a quiet, distraction-free environment. This is usually before e-mails begin filling inboxes, phones begin ringing, and people want to chat about things that need to be accomplished.
- Midday: either close the office door, turn off all notifications, and make it known that disruptions are not welcome or leave the office to go somewhere quiet where distractions will not interfere with work.
- Evening: Stay a couple hours after everyone else leaves the office so there are no distractions.

Similarly, take time at home when it is quiet to get a couple hours of deep work done.

The time of day chosen for deep work depends on when someone has the time and energy to focus. It is important to note the time of day when one can be most productive and schedule deep work for that time. [45] If someone is not productive first thing in the morning, then going into the office early to do deep work is not a good idea.

Newport's last method of accomplishing deep work is the journalistic method. This method requires fitting deep work into one's schedule whenever it can be for as long or short a time as one is able. Although this method might initially sound like the ideal approach, it requires the ability to focus quickly and easily as one transitions from one task to another. [46] This means that one must already be practiced at focusing on a single task in order for it to be as effective as possible. Without the neural pathways necessary for focus, one will simply struggle to accomplish deep work in this way as they struggle against external and internal distractions in addition to the residual thoughts from the previous task.

The approach one chooses to integrate deep work into their life will depend on their needs, schedule, job, and home life. For a person with children at home, the monastic method will rarely work, if it works at all. The rhythmic and journalistic methods, however, are much easier to work into a life with many ongoing responsibilities. Whichever method someone chooses, once their brain is trained to accomplish deep work, they will see results as their work showcases their skills, talents, and potential.

Essentialism Complements Deep Work

Melding essentialism with deep work is another crucial component in setting boundaries to be productive and happy at work. The two approaches to work complement one another, working together to maximize time spent on work that contributes to personal and company goals. Essentialism is a term coined by Greg McKeown to describe an attitude that manifests in spending time on only the things that are important to one's role at work. This isn't about doing less for the sake of doing less, or even about working fewer hours. Essentialism is about targeting time and energy toward the projects that will benefit the most from the strengths, skills, and talents a person has. McKeown calls this a person's "highest point of contribution." [47]

It means saying no to anything that does not allow one to achieve their potential within their role. Whenever a new project, request, or task is proposed, it must be weighed against the available resources, available time, and one's ability to contribute meaningfully to their career and the company. For example, if someone's role is to redesign processes that need improvement because of their analytical abilities and attention to detail, a budget meeting will not provide the opportunity for them to shine. Their skills are not needed. Essentialism suggests the person not attend the meeting. Instead, they focus on the project that will allow them to contribute best.

Mckeown suggests everything that comes across one's path, in work and in life, needs to be weighed with this criterion. In this way, people can avoid the stress that comes with taking on too many responsibilities. At the same time, it makes room in a calendar for someone to spend time and energy exploring other options within their skill set, ultimately making work (and life) easier.

In addition to finding work easier and more satisfying, people can create a sense of control for themselves, focusing on meaningful work, and setting boundaries that allow them to be productive and grow their skills within the parameters of their job. People find new energy and motivation as they complete tasks and prioritize ahead of time, effectively avoiding the common condition of burnout.

When a person couples essentialism with periods of deep work, they give themselves the time and space to be creative within their skill set and their passion, to push the boundaries of what they have currently achieved, and to move beyond the surface level of problems or projects. They can grow their talents to create transformative work rather than simply getting the bare minimum done—they do "less but better." [48]

To truly achieve these results through a life of essentialism, a person must learn to say "no" to things that do not align with their highest point of

contribution. This, however, is not always an easy thing
to do.

Saying "No"

Saying no can be terrifying at first. Society has trained
people to say "yes" to managers, bosses, friends, and
family. People are applauded for doing so much, piling
their plates high, and taking on more and more projects.
Stress becomes a badge of honor that displays how much
someone can accomplish–until they can't accomplish
anything anymore. It is important to start saying no
before reaching the point of exhaustion, hopelessness,
and frustration.

It is important to remember that as scary as it might be to
start answering in the negative, answering "yes" might
have greater negative consequences. If someone is
already stretched too thin, they may not have the capacity
to accomplish a new task to the best of their ability. In the
attempt to complete the task, they may make mistakes or
oversights that compromise the quality of the work or
harm the relationship and ultimately their reputation. [49]
Instead of cultivating value within a working relationship
or within the company, saying yes could actually produce
the opposite result. With this in mind, saying "no" might
feel easier.

Answering in the negative, however, is not as simple as
uttering the single word, "no." It must be done with
intention, compassion, and grace. People being refused
need to clearly understand that taking on an extra

responsibility will be detrimental to the company by taking away the time and energy needed for a different project. They don't need a detailed and patronizing explanation, just a sentence that lets them know prioritizing their request is not possible at this time. It might even be helpful to offer an alternative solution by suggesting another person who is better suited to the role. It is also helpful to let them know you might be willing to help in the future. Any of the following examples can be diplomatic and assertive ways to say "no."

- I would love to help with your project, but right now I need to give my attention to redesigning the marketing strategy before the next board meeting.
- I wish I could help, but this project is not my strength. Zain might be a great choice to help you with this one.
- That sounds like something I'd love to help with, but my calendar is full for the next few weeks. Maybe I'll be able to help next time around.

There may be some initial shock that the immediate response is not agreement, but saying no demonstrates a strong ability to prioritize, great time management skills, and clear communication. Saying no will not devalue an employee if there is a reason behind the answer that will ultimately benefit the company.

Once someone begins saying no so they can focus on what is essential at work, they can begin to train themselves to accomplish deep work. People can genuinely focus on producing quality work that exceeds previous standards because they aren't distracted by many other menial tasks. With deep work comes more productivity with greater quality since one is not required to do more with less but less with more. People can take projects further than they could before, offering innovation, creativity, thoughtfulness, and skill to each project. Their value as employees will rise, and they will begin to see their passion reignite as they spend time on tasks they feel are meaningful. [50] Essentialism melded with deep work allows people to work smarter, not harder and longer. Adjectives like efficient, versatile, productive, motivated, ambitious, reliable, focused, committed, team player, and adept will be used to describe these employees, and they will have been achieved without risking burnout, incredible stress, or the quality of the work.

Action Steps

Identify a time when you feel most productive, and set that time aside for a single important task each day. Start with one hour to begin training your brain to focus. When you get to that time, shut your office door, reduce distractions, turn off your phone, e-mail notifications, and any other notifications you have set, and focus on the task at hand. Slowly increase the amount of time you dedicate to this time of deep work.

Similarly, identify a time of day when you feel less productive and incapable of your best work. Dedicate that time to shallow work so your day is divided into time for deep work and time for shallow work.

Take a moment to write down your point of highest contribution. Put this somewhere it is visible and use it to weigh the tasks on your to-do list or the ones that come across your desk. When there are tasks that do not allow you to contribute in your areas of strength, cross them off your to-do list, or practice saying "no" assertively and with grace. These steps will lead you toward greater productivity, less exhaustion, and reduced stress.

Chapter Summary

- Society that praises busyness and stress, believing this makes people successful and productive.
- Most of the workday is filled with shallow work, leaving little time for work that offers value to careers and companies.
- A plate filled with meaningless tasks leads to higher stress levels and, eventually, burnout.
- Burnout is common but avoidable.
- Deep work and essentialism are key components for productivity and success.

4

THE POWER OF THE PAUSE

HOW GIVING YOUR BRAIN A BREAK CAN SUPERCHARGE YOUR DECISION-MAKING PROWESS

M ichelle considered herself productive at work; she always completed everything on her to-do list, even if it rarely showcased her best work. She volunteered for projects and presentations before anyone else, earning a reputation as a go-getter. Everyone seemed to be satisfied with her work, even if she wasn't. She rarely took a lunch break, preferring working lunches to maximize her time. It was easy to accomplish the little things on her to-do list, but it was becoming challenging to complete the more significant projects, and she found herself slipping in the details. Michelle knew it was only a matter of time before she could no longer live up to her reputation. So, she increased her work hours, and it was solving her problem, but she was too exhausted to do anything when she got home. Her meals of chips on the couch while scrolling through her phone or Netflix were becoming more common.

Michelle told herself she was tired because she needed to go to bed earlier and eat better, but somehow she never managed to make it between the sheets any earlier. Instead of making healthier meals at home, she got takeout on her way home from work. She justified that choice with thoughts of saving time and energy, but she never seemed to have any more of either time or energy. When she was presented with the option of higher rent or moving out, she was too tired to look for a new apartment. So, she told herself the extra few hundred dollars a month was worth it for the space and location.

It wasn't until Michelle's company suffered financially and let her go that she realized she had not developed the skills other employers sought. Instead of spending time cultivating her talents or learning from the leaders of her industry, Michelle focused on the little tasks that were easy to complete. Anyone else could do what she had spent years doing. She knew she was not remarkable in her industry; Michelle was simply good at being busy.

Now, she found herself stuck at home, not knowing what to do next. While driving to dinner at her parent's office, the radio show she listened to featured a segment on the importance of rest. She decided the next step was to take some time to rest and reflect.

Over the next month, Michelle took time to notice the world around her. She went on walks, spent time with her family, hired a career coach, and began to do mindful meditation. During this time, she realized the pride she felt at perceived productivity stemmed from her need for approval and that her fear of failure held her back from learning to be invaluable in the industry.

The time and space away from the busy world gave Michelle a chance to think and reflect, solve her internal problems that manifested externally, and refocus her priorities. She felt calmer, more confident, and more competent. She spent some time reading and learning about the trajectory of her field while continuing her newfound habits.

When Michelle found another job, she brought this new knowledge and attitude. She could give more to her career because she was refreshed and maintained habits of rest. She prioritized more easily, had greater clarity about her goals and how her work aligned with them, and became valuable to the company and the industry. Michelle even had the energy to find a new apartment, so she wasn't paying as much in rent, and she created healthy meal plans so she wasn't getting take-out each night.

Like Michelle, many people live under the pressure of false productivity. They are expected to get more done than they have time for, to post accomplishments on social media, and to watch as people like and comment on that perceived success. What society has yet to realize is that real success requires times of rest. Spring cannot come without the dormancy of winter. Winters provide rest, recovery, and refreshment. [1] Katherine May beautifully describes taking time to do this as "deeply unfashionable" but necessary in a world that admires constant busyness. It is by taking time and space that we "shed a skin…expose all those painful nerve endings and feel so raw that [we'll] need to take care of [ourselves] for a while." If we don't do this, our "skin will harden around" us. [2] Without quiet times, people cannot move forward. Far from holding a person back, resting propels them toward their goals.

Reframing Boredom

Almost everyone has groaned and complained about being bored at some point in their lives. Boredom isn't new and isn't contained in a single country. It is a universal experience that people have complained about for centuries. The definition of boredom has changed over time from something akin to the deadly sin of slothfulness to an illness of sorts and, most recently, to a feeling associated with a lack of stimulation. [3] What has remained common throughout the ages is that boredom has been viewed as a negative emotion. In the current world, boredom is avoided in every way possible by filling calendars with activities, outings, social media, and streaming services. No one wants to have a quiet moment where the possibility of feeling bored looms.

Studies have shown that boredom is associated with mental health issues, drug and alcohol abuse, and even that it complicates the healing process in brain trauma. Boredom leaves people listless, lost in a purposeless existence that, if not dealt with, can result in feelings of a total loss of control over one's life and an inability to identify what they actually want to be doing in their life. If boredom is inconvenient and dangerous, it is no wonder society views it as terrible. But what if the perspective on boredom changed?

Researchers are beginning to argue that boredom is "an issue of attention" rather than an emotion. [4] When someone pays attention to something with focus, they connect with a part of their world meaningfully. [5] If someone has trouble giving something attention, they struggle to connect with it and find purpose in the activity. They do not feel compelled to carry on the activity, and instead experience the desire for it to be over. There is no mental or emotional engagement, and the person is bored. In light of this information, boredom can be seen as a tool for growth and success.

Some theorists suggest that boredom is akin to disgust–the desire to immediately remove oneself from something repulsive. This theory doesn't seem too wild when considering that centuries ago, boredom was thought of as an illness, a feeling of nausea, something a person felt when disgusted. Today, someone might say they are "sick of this" when they find themselves in a situation that is not as interesting or in a cycle they can't escape in their daily lives. In this frame, boredom is a warning sign, telling someone to avoid something potentially harmful.

If a person finds that they are bored at home every night of the week, unsure of what to do with themselves, boredom might be a sign of a more serious problem. For example, they might be bored because they are struggling to carve a social life out of their busy schedule, often ending up too exhausted to do anything, like Michelle. If the pattern continues, the issue can lead to mental health issues from lack of work-life balance and isolation. The feeling of boredom can signal the possibility of the problem compounding. If it is paid attention to as such, it can be the first step to realizing a change must happen to avoid bigger and more difficult issues.

When someone identifies the feeling of boredom at work, the same principle can be applied. This feeling implies a lack of engagement with this part of their world; they do not feel inspired or motivated by their projects, and the boredom is a signal they need projects that will capture their attention. This may be a result of a lack of agency in their jobs, an excess of shallow work, or filling their schedule with work that doesn't challenge and grow their skills to allow for their highest point of contribution. If the boredom is not remedied, the likelihood of experiencing burnout increases. Identifying the cause of it can help someone move forward in their life rather than remaining stagnant. In order to take this step, though, one must become comfortable with boredom instead of perceiving it as a negative emotion that is remedied by filling time.

Once the perspective on boredom shifts, it might actually become a positive thing, and the desire to fill time with busyness or distractions) will no longer rule the moment when boredom occurs. In fact, when one becomes comfortable with being bored, they might even seek out moments of boredom in their search for areas of improvement. They may find they become more present in their world, and that sometimes boredom isn't a warning sign, but rather a moment in life where calendars aren't entirely filled with projects, activities, and meetings. These times may have been mistaken for boredom and under closer examination, they offer time to slow down and recuperate before the next season of intense industrious effort.

Taking Time & Space

It is easy to get caught up in the whirlwind of life. People often forget that taking time to rest, reflect, recharge, and center themselves is as important as the other tasks on their to-do lists. People often go from one meeting to the next with no time between them, rushing to use the little time they have to accomplish as much as possible. This is, after all, efficiency and productivity at its best. This type of constant activity is deemed not just acceptable but praiseworthy. The working parent wearing multiple hats is admired, while the businessperson constantly on the run is viewed as successful and valuable. In addition to busy days, many people end their workday with the next task on their minds and all the things they didn't finish that day. Society exists in a never-ending busyness that doesn't allow much rest. People might sit in front of the television at the end of the day and think this is their time to rest and relax, to zone out and not focus on anything. Or, after two long meetings in a row, someone might feel they deserve a social media break at work and spend thirty minutes checking in with colleagues and friends online, supplying themselves with a needed release of dopamine in an otherwise enjoyable day. Far from offering recuperation, screen time distractions inhibit a person's ability to live a productive and happy life. Instead, they perpetuate bad habits and distractions and, even worse, alter how the brain works, leading to a low sense of well-being. What people actually need is a good break between times of high stress and high performance.

Microsoft released a recent study on beta brain waves measuring stress levels in meeting participants. [6] They split their small number of participants into two groups, one of which was given no breaks between back-to-back meetings. The other was given ten-minute breaks, or "buffer space," between meetings. Each group wore electroencephalogram equipment to measure brain activity throughout and between the meetings. The participants with no breaks showed higher levels of stress activity in the brain and stress levels that increased as time went on. These people were not given time to rest and reset from the stress of one meeting, and knowing they had no time to transition before their next meeting raised their stress levels. The participants with breaks between meetings showed more stable brain activity and no accumulating stress as they approached the next meeting. These participants also demonstrated greater engagement in the meetings, allowing them to participate meaningfully in the discussions.

Although not a peer-reviewed scientific study, the results are hard to argue. It is clear that breaks from the hustle and stress are essential for health and well-being. Simply taking note of how one feels in the middle of a busy day lets them know a break is needed. This study, however, clearly reveals that more than a lunch break is required to reset and refocus. People must take small breaks between high-level performances and activities throughout the day. These smaller and more frequent breaks give time and space to recharge between tasks, allowing people to give the best of their skill in each job while ensuring they do not run into decision fatigue.

It is important to note that as part of Microsoft's study, the participants given breaks were not merely allowed to do whatever they wanted; they were required to meditate using the Headspace app, an app designed to lead users through various meditations to reduce stress, promote relaxation, and improve sleep. This detail is of note because studies are beginning to show that focused rest is what not only resets stress levels but trains the brain to be active in important ways that ultimately improve mental health and productivity. Instead of sitting in front of the television or computer for a break, people need focused rest to recharge.

Focused Rest Vs. Non-Focused Rest

Focused rest does not mean sitting in front of the television concentrating on a film or show. It does not mean focusing on the latest drama unfolding in social media feeds or playing video games that help a person zone out of the world around them, alleviating stress and anxiety. Focused rest also does not mean rest with no focus on a particular thing. Instead, it means purposeful time and space to be mindful of what one is feeling and what is happening in their thoughts.

When given time to rest without a focus, the brain activity moves into the default mode network (DMN). [7] This part of the brain becomes active when attention shifts from a particular task to "mind-wandering" or "daydreaming." [8] Although people may enjoy their daydreams as cathartic experiences for many of their frustrations, daydreams ultimately do not benefit productivity. Mind-wandering is seen in people whose attention is not successfully engaged in meaningful activity. [9] This means that daydreaming is a sign that someone is likely experiencing a lack of control, passion, and purpose in their lives at that moment. Essentially, they are bored of where they are at in life. When these feelings continue for more extended periods, more severe problems can arise. This "discontinuity of mind" is associated with a lack of comfort (both inner and environmental) and correlates with mental illness and a lack of well-being. [10] People who experience anxiety and depression are more likely to experience discontinuity of mind and discomfort during unfocused rest periods. Those who experience prolonged or frequent unfocused rest periods that do not engage their attention meaningfully have higher instances of "displeasure, sadness, emptiness, anxiety," and anger. [11]

On the opposite end of the spectrum, those who feel they generally have a high level of mental well-being are more likely to experience comfort during a rest period and an ability to focus on their physical environment, self-awareness, and directed planning. [12] In other words, control over one's thoughts and purposeful attention to external and internal stimuli positively correlate with mental health and well-being.

Sitting down in a quiet space for only a moment with no direct focus can make the brain active in the DMN. If someone already feels anxiety, depression, or hopelessness, rest without a specific focus can enhance these states rather than provide much-needed alleviation. This is where focused rest becomes one of the best tools to help with decision fatigue and the accompanying symptoms.

Focused Rest Through Mindful Meditation

Focused rest can be achieved in various ways, but mindful meditation is one of the most common and effective. Like mindfulness exercises, mindful meditation helps a person focus on the present in a way that calms rather than increases stress. Unlike mindfulness exercises, which can be achieved anywhere during almost any activity, mindful meditation is purposeful time set aside to focus on a particular aspect of a person's present moment. This method of focused rest will not only provide the focused rest that can help reset the brain, increasing productivity and alleviating decision fatigue but will also improve one's general sense of well-being.

One of the known sources of stimulation for the DMN is "spontaneous self-related mentation" focused on the past or the future. [13] These thoughts are usually related to worry, fear, and anxiety as minds wander within these subjects. Rarely are these thoughts focused on solutions or actions to address fears. Instead, thoughts can spiral, sending someone further into distracted and unproductive thought patterns that characterize mental health and well-being challenges. [14] When thinking back to the information about external and internal distractions, this information solidifies the need to focus on the present.

Mindful meditation often begins with what is called "focused attention meditation." [15] This type of meditation is practiced by directing attention to a chosen experience, like the sensations experienced with each breath a person takes. Someone could also focus on a mantra or a phrase they want to internalize that day. For example, someone feeling particularly stressed may focus on the phrase, "I accept what I cannot change, and I am calm and present in the face of uncertainty" as they breathe deeply. The attention focused on something specific, instead of letting the mind wander into distraction, is a crucial part of the practice. Whether a person focuses on the sensation of breathing, a body scan, or a mantra the results of the focused meditation will be the same. [16] Under this focused attention, the brain activity moves from the DMN into other areas of the brain that allow for the development of focused attention in a particular task. [17] Development of this skill is critical in a world where people's brains are trained to constantly switch gears, moving from one task to the next or even between two or three jobs simultaneously. As Cal Newport describes in *Deep Work*, living with the distractions deemed normal and even necessary results in an inability to focus. [18] Focused attention meditation can be a wonderful way to retrain the brain to become more productive and less distracted.

As practitioners become more adept at focused attention meditation, they can move more quickly into mindful meditation. Often these two methods are combined in traditional meditation practices, allowing those who practice refining their skills. [19] Mindful meditation involves more than simply being aware of the present moment or focusing on a single thing. Instead, the goal of mindful meditation is to observe oneself, one's mind, and one's surroundings in an objective, and ultimately detached way, while breathing. There is no specific focus, rather a concentration on what is happening internally and externally in the moment of meditation. The expectation is that these internal and external experiences are acknowledged with no judgment and then let go as the practitioner continues to breathe and focus on whatever the next internal experience. In this way, there is no emotional reaction to the feelings that surface during the meditation, simply an acknowledgment of them, ultimately creating neural pathways for emotional regulation. The ultimate goal of mindful meditation is to achieve a sense of self that is separate from the external and internal experiences of the practitioner. [20] This separation enables an objective perspective of the world that accepts events, people, thoughts, and emotions without the judgments that can cause stress. When emotions are regulated in this way, there is less energy spent on reacting to them, and more energy available for other things. In addition, with less rumination, depression and anxiety are reduced, increasing one's sense of well-being. [21]

Part of emotional regulation related to mindfulness is acknowledging how one feels rather than finding an escape from those feelings by another means. People often look for a release of dopamine to avoid their emotions in the present moment or to avoid feeling uncomfortable about whatever issue they are facing. This is where people often move to social media, checking how many likes or views they have on posts or how many comments have been made. This is also where a lack of impulse control takes over, and people do whatever feels best at that moment, often leading to further distraction, procrastination, or unproductive behavior. These impulses can be avoided when people notice how they feel and what they might need due to those feelings. They can respond appropriately rather than react to the feelings because they are aware and because more areas of the brain interact and engage in the process than just the DMN.

Something interesting to note is the release of dopamine when people practice loving kindness meditation. [22] Loving kindness meditation (LKM) involves a general feeling or wish of goodwill, love, and compassion toward self and others. When this becomes a genuine feeling during LKM, it activates the dopamine system, which is part of the reward and motivation response. This means that instead of caving to a tempting distraction, one can instead engage in a short loving kindness meditation. They will then not only receive the reward and motivation accompanying the release of dopamine, but they will also experience greater emotional regulation while practicing their ability to focus and activate other areas of the brain. This experience and practice will not draw from finite energy stores but will help reenergize and reset the brain to tackle the tasks ahead.

Emotional regulation is not the only benefit meditators experience. The less energy it takes to move from distraction to focus, the easier it is for the brain to switch between tasks, focus, control inhibitions, remember, and plan. [23] Having an easier time doing all these things means more energy can be spent on other tasks or engaging in deep work.

The results of increased brain activity in multiple areas are not limited to experienced practitioners of traditional meditation; even novice practitioners can experience the benefits of meditation. Remember that the key to these benefits is focused attention that moves brain activity from the DMN into other areas of the brain. This can be accomplished through non-traditional forms of meditation as people pick a specific focus to bring their attention to. Although not scientifically proven, Cal Newport's idea of "productive meditation" draws the focus away from mind-wandering and brings it to a specific focus. [24]

"Productive Meditation"

Like traditional meditation, "productive meditation" requires practice and patience. It is not an easy task, but there will be greater productivity from deep work with fortitude and perseverance.

Previously, deep work was described as time set aside to work on a single specific task that requires time, attention, and focus. It is a task that cannot be completed while distracted or in a short time. Phones must be put away or turned off, notifications must be silenced, and space must be quiet so one can remain undisturbed during the time they have set aside. This is not the only way to accomplish deep work, however. Productive meditation is a way to practice deep work without needing time and space apart from other aspects of the day.

Productive meditation is an extension of deep work. Newport suggests one can enter into a period of intense focus while doing something else. It melds productivity and efficiency with elements of traditional meditation to help people achieve more extraordinary things in work and life. "Productive meditation" is done while doing something physically active that doesn't require mental engagement. [25] This chosen activity is going to be different for everyone. Some people like to jog while practicing this type of deep work; however, if someone is not an experienced runner, their brain will need to focus on the physical activity of running or breathing rather than the mental activity required for productive meditation. Instead, a walk or a bike ride may work well. Newport even suggests productive meditation can happen while showering. The activity doesn't matter as much as a person's ability to perform it without thinking. Many people do it while stuck in their car during rush hour traffic. It is also important to remember that since "productive meditation" aims to enter into a place of deep work, one needs to disengage as many distractions as possible. For example, it is not likely a person will have their phone in the shower, notifying them of all new activities happening in their world. Similarly, distractions should be minimal if engaged in "productive meditation" during a run, a bike ride, or at the gym. Leaving phones and music behind is critical to this concept. Once someone has chosen the best activity to engage in this practice, the next step is identifying what they need to focus on.

Whether a person chooses to outline a piece of writing for work, plan a presentation, or solve a problem they face, their choice becomes the goal for the "productive meditation" session that day. This goal is what they come back to over and over again whenever they become distracted, applying the principles of traditional meditation of focusing on a single thought or sensation at a time and being mindful, at the moment, of where their thoughts are moving. As soon as they move away from the focal point, they gently bring themselves back to it without criticizing themselves for being distracted. At first, the mind might wander to problems unrelated to the chosen focus, like the leak in the roof that needs fixing or the garden work that keeps piling up as the weather gets warmer. It is easy to notice these distracted thoughts and to refocus. As someone becomes more proficient at "productive meditation," the distracted thoughts become more nuanced.

For example, thoughts may end up "looping." This means someone begins to think about things they have already thought about and know regarding the chosen focus. They get stuck reviewing the same thoughts and information rather than moving deeper into the subject matter. [26] As with the deep work sessions discussed in chapter two, this process aims to bring people to new places of thought, challenge thinking, come up with new ideas and solutions, and inspire creativity to bring something new and effective to the table. If a person ends up ruminating over what they already know, they cannot take their work to the next level. If "looping" happens during productive meditation, the solution is the same as with a more obvious distraction: recognize the distraction and then refocus on the initial issue. [27] It can help to have a few purposeful questions on hand to help move from looping into deep work. For example, when one notices that they are simply reviewing what is already known or completed, they can ask themselves one of the following questions:

- What is the next step in this process?

- What is one possible roadblock, and how can I avoid it?
- Who is my audience/client, and what is important to them? How can I meet their need while keeping that in mind?
- What steps do I need to take next to achieve my goal in this project?

The questions will be unique to each person and each focus, but the list above can help move someone forward when caught in a loop. They will take them deeper into the problem and eventually allow them to accomplish the goals of deep work.

Creating a specific structure for productive meditation sessions will help maintain focus and move someone forward into deep work. With the identified focus, one must determine the most important question regarding that focus. Do they need to solve a problem? If so, they need to outline all the aspects of that issue to begin solving it. If they are planning a presentation or other project, they need to identify the key elements and explore the possibilities for each component individually. [28] Ensuring the time is structured during "productive meditation" will help keep one on track while ensuring they move beyond the surface level of the problem.

Newport explains two critical steps when the session ends: review the progress from the session and leave the focus of the meditation to unconscious thought. [29], [30] To solidify the progress made during "productive meditation," it is essential to note the discoveries made, the questions asked or even answered, and the main points learned by scouring the point of focus. [31] Taking the time to complete this step at the end of the process helps people remember the next time they need to focus deeply on the subject. It also avoids repeating any of the process or thoughts, thereby gaining maximum efficiency and productivity. Depending on which activity someone has chosen to do while productively meditating, they may want to have their phone ready to record these notes or a notebook and pen handy to write this information down.

Once the necessary information from the session is recorded, the rest is left to the Unconscious Thought Theory. [32] This theory states that as the brain is consciously focused on something, the unconscious mind continues to ruminate on a current problem and how to solve it. Essentially, Newport suggests that once a productive meditation is complete, a person can sit back and let the unconscious mind do the work. The mind continues to work through the problem, reviewing the points from the session and coming up with solutions and ideas to take the work to the next level. The next time someone can focus on the problem, they will be further ahead than where they left off.

It takes time and practice to become effective at productive meditation (just as it does with traditional meditation), and making it a regular part of the week will help with mastering this skill. Working at this will also help develop the focus necessary for deep work sessions scheduled throughout the week. [33] Productive meditation can be worked into a weekly schedule along with a form of traditional meditation to reap the benefits of both for maximum efficiency, productivity, emotional regulation, and well-being and to avoid decision fatigue and burnout. Meditative practices are not the only ones people can apply to accomplish a greater sense of well-being and to create time and space for themselves in their daily lives. Creating clear boundaries between work and home can help with this process, too.

The "Shutdown Ritual"

Separating from the demands of pressing problems by leaving them to the unconscious is more important than ever when the lines between work and home are blurred. E-mail notifications continue to go off during evenings at home or on the weekends, and many people pack a work bag to bring their laptops home to continue working at home. Many people feel the need to take this extra time to complete the workload that has piled up over the week. This is a mistake that leads to exhaustion and burnout. Instead, it is essential to separate oneself from work and take the time and space to relax, take care of oneself, and let the brain rest and reset as much as possible. This is a form of space between periods of intense work. Each evening can function as a rest, providing time and space to recuperate.

It can be difficult to achieve this separation, so making the separation purposeful is one way to ensure it happens.

Cognitive behavioral psychologists suggest an activity that delineates two activities. This allows people to disconnect from one part of their lives to fully move into the next with no residual attention focused on the previous activity. These routines are especially beneficial during times of change and stress. [34] They are purposeful moments in the day that bring a person into the present, create a sense of mindfulness, and signify that work is complete and the time now exists for a different activity. [35] Cal Newport takes this to heart, and his "shutdown ritual" has become famous.

Newport has created an end-of-day ritual that encompasses all of these elements and ensures he is not distracted by a to-do list throughout his evening. He goes through this process at the end of every workday at a set time. The first step of his practice is to update his task list. He adds anything new from the day and ensures he removes anything that he has accomplished. He then reads over the list and sets due dates for anything that feels more important or urgent than the other tasks. [36] Creating due dates will ensure these tasks appear in a calendar, and notifications will be sent to remind one of those deadlines. The assistance of these electronic tools takes one more responsibility off one's shoulders and becomes one less thing to worry about at work and at home.

Newport then reviews his calendar for the next couple of weeks to ensure he knows what is coming up and can plan accordingly. He understands that schedules and appointments change throughout the day, so it is necessary to review them on a daily basis. He uses this information to update his weekly plan, make any changes that need to be made, or create notations about what he accomplished that day. [37] Newport's to-do list for the next day is completed in these practices. This means that he doesn't have to think about it at home, but it also means he doesn't need to begin the next workday with decisions about prioritizing tasks. It is already done, reducing the energy he needs to expend on decision-making.

The final step of Newport's "shutdown ritual" is to say, "Schedule shutdown, complete." [38] Although this may seem unnatural and even uncomfortable to some people, the spoken finality of the phrase effectively does what behavioral psychology suggests in disconnecting from one aspect of life to allow movement into the next with mindfulness and focus on the present. Newport says that after he utters this phrase, he can remind himself that the shutdown is complete if he finds himself still engaged about a topic or worry connected to work. He has already completed the most important tasks to organize himself for what comes next when he gets back to work. There is nothing he needs to worry about regarding this topic.

Just as any meditation takes practice, so does separating life at work from life outside of work. A person must break habits of worry, rumination, and distraction that impact their ability to function at their best. Behaviors in end-of-day routines don't have to be the same as Newport's. Each person needs to find something that works for them. It will be helpful to ensure to-do lists are made at the end of the day so that time and energy are not spent doing that the next day. Having those decisions made ahead of time makes a significant difference in productivity and allows one to jump right into the most important task when they are fresh the next day. However, whatever the transition behaviors someone chooses to implement, the behaviors should denote a clear separation. Some people begin by shutting down each program on their computer before powering it off. Others make a phone call to a colleague or friend to signify the end of their workday. [39] An effective strategy for a commuter might be to create a playlist of songs that will help them transition into the attitude they need or want for the next part of their day. This might be songs about letting go of one thing, or it might be songs about moving on to something different. It might be songs about the weekend and relaxing on a Friday night. Each person will need to find something that works best for them. Then, once that transitional behavior is done, they must commit to not looking back or forward to the next day at work.

This time and space give the brain time to rest, reset, and refocus. And don't worry, the unconscious mind is never at rest. It will still be working while someone spends a relaxing evening doing whatever they do when they aren't working.

<u>What Do I Do Now?</u>

In a world that never seems to stop, it can be difficult for people to figure out what to do once they have left work and the busyness behind. Figuring out this step is just as important as any of the other information discussed so far.

Greg McKeown tells people to "discover the art of doing nothing. Do not do more today than you can completely recover from tomorrow." [40] What "nothing" means is different for everyone. The most important part is understanding the pressure to be busy, productive, and efficient constantly. The lie exists that people fail if they don't consistently achieve something great. This simply isn't true.

"The art of nothing" means one can feel comfortable not producing measurable results. Instead, they can relax and enjoy the moment. This might mean sitting in the sun on a deck while watching the wind sway the branches of nearby trees. It may mean conversing with a friend while drinking a glass of wine and eating on a patio. While it may feel that someone is not being productive, they are allowing their bodies and minds to rest. They also may be building relationships and giving time, energy, and attention to the people they care about, including themselves. They are cultivating a life where they have time for themselves and their families and feel a sense of fulfillment, peace, and well-being.

Action Steps

When we live lives full of work and activities that create a constant busyness, it is hard to carve time out of that to give ourselves a rest. This makes it even more important to plan for it.

Start by scheduling five to ten minutes between tasks or meetings to rest and reset. Use the Headspace app (or a similar one) to help you meditate for a few minutes to reset your brain and reduce stress if you struggle to achieve a mindfulness mindset.

Think about what you can do before leaving work to help alleviate stress about your to-do list and create a plan for the following day. Then come up with a behavior that signals the transition from work to life outside of work and do it at the end of every day. When this transition activity is done, you can leave work in the office and focus on doing something that allows for enjoyable rest. Remind yourself that boredom isn't harmful but a tool for growth and success.

With these steps, you will notice a difference in how you feel and your productivity in the time allotted to work.

Chapter Summary

- If perceived differently, boredom can be a tool rather than a hindrance.
- The brain needs time and space to process and reset between tasks, especially those that require deep thinking and intense focus, in order to work efficiently.

- Meditation trains the brain to be more efficient, allowing one to expend less energy on emotional regulation, change, and decision-making.
- "Productive meditation" is a practice that engages someone in deep work while simultaneously accomplishing something physical that they need to do anyway.
- End-of-day routines are essential in disentangling from work and allowing one to reset for the next day, an essential step in avoiding burnout.

5

MAKE BETTER DECISIONS THROUGH FOCUS

HOW TO NAVIGATE DISTRACTIONS AND CULTIVATE LASER-FOCUSED DECISION-MAKING

W hat if we could completely change our lives with only a few minor tweaks to our daily routine? Consider the impact of not checking our phone and e-mail notifications when we wake up. Instead, we can jump into our morning routine without distraction, without decisions, and without emotional responses to whatever we find on our phone first thing in the morning. We would have more energy going through our morning and a greater focus on whatever is on the agenda for the morning. We wouldn't be accessing our energy reserves or decision bank first thing in the morning, which would prepare us for whatever unexpected events might occur that day.

Imagine, instead of checking our phones, we replaced that activity with a five-minute meditation that helped us regulate our emotions and focus our brain, opening neural pathways and connections needed for the day ahead, and released dopamine resulting in energy and motivation for what was to come. We would be purposefully setting ourselves up for a day of success.

When it comes to social media, screens, and technology, people are usually on board with setting limits for children. They can easily acknowledge the damage and distraction these things can cause in the lives of others, making comments about addiction, unrealistic expectations, and the demand to keep up with the platforms and the trends. However, people often fail to recognize these impacts in their own lives, and they fail to set limits for themselves. If for different reasons, it is as important to set boundaries for oneself as it is to set limits for others or children. Implementing technology restrictions to help prevent distractions will help move one away from the fatigue and burnout they experience. They will help one effectively fight decision fatigue. These minor limitations will move someone into productivity and greater well-being.

External Distractions

As discussed in chapter two, people face an incredible number of distractions every day. The technological tools many people require to complete their jobs can quickly become distractions with a constant flow of notifications, the temptation to check social media, e-mails in inboxes, and news updates. The physical space a person is in can even be a distraction. Each of these distractions can consume attention and energy, causing someone to be less productive. They pull from one's limited energy stores as they make choices about each of them, impacting their ability to make decisions later in the day. There is also the danger of these diversions contributing to the decline of mental health with consequences of anxiety, depression, hopelessness, and frustration. It is increasingly important for each person to be aware of these distractions in their lives and effectively combat them to improve productivity and mental health. Managing these intrusions will help avoid burnout and decision fatigue.

Technology

Technology surrounds people in nearly every aspect of their lives. There certainly are benefits as it offers a wide range of tools that can be used to make jobs easier and faster, provides space for information sharing, and gives people easy access to their world and customer base. Without limits, however, it blurs the lines between tool and hindrance.

Setting limits on technology use can feel difficult and counterproductive. But if someone looks honestly at how they use technology, they can determine how to set personal limits to ensure it remains a tool rather than a distraction. They must step back from their phones, computers, e-mails, and social media to take an objective look at how they use them throughout the day. When the level of personal engagement with these technologies is determined, prioritizing time and attention is easier. If, for example, someone realizes they check social media and personal messages throughout the day, they can decide that turning off all personal notifications will help them focus. Determining why they check their devices throughout the day is also essential. Is it out of a habit they need to break, or does it result from the need to feel a sense of positivity and joy on an otherwise arduous day? If it is the latter, one can decide how else they might accomplish the same goal. Perhaps a five-minute meditation, a walk outside, or even a quick chat with a colleague will achieve the same effect while functioning as a short rest period. People also might find that putting time aside for deep work will give them a sense of accomplishment that satisfies that need.

It isn't always easy to introspectively determine the reason behind habits and behaviors. However, without this step, a person cannot effectively move out of the places they find themselves stuck in their lives. This process of self-awareness will help set limits that work to move one into productivity, efficiency, and well-being.

One of the ways to set these limits is by putting phones and computers away at the end of the day and leaving them until a predetermined time the next morning. For example, someone may want to leave these devices in a drawer with all notifications turned off for the night so that they do not tempt them. If they are not available first thing in the morning, they are less likely to check them when they wake up. Instead, they can get ready for the day without technology distractions. This may allow them to leave for the office earlier with a clear mind, or it might enable them to enjoy time with their family rather than rushing out of the house. This limit can be even more effective if a time is set to put phones and computers away in the evening. Setting a nightly reminder to put a device away is one way to ensure not forget this step. Someone might even decide to put their devices away when they get home from work, ensuring their evening is free of any distractions that take away their ability to delineate work from home.

If someone checks their phone often throughout the work day, creating a schedule can help solve this issue. Within this schedule, they can designate times to check devices, put them away, and focus on other tasks, like deep work. They may even extend this schedule beyond the workday to include events and tasks outside of work, helping to keep them accountable to limiting their technology use at home, too. Everyone's day looks different, and everyone has unique needs, preferences, and motivations. So, each person's schedule must be personalized to work for them. This schedule should emerge from self-reflection and honest assessment of one's tendencies. The following work schedule is an example of what could be useful for someone struggling with the constant distraction of their devices.

Time	Event
8:00 am - 9:55 am	Deep work: presentation for Friday's meeting
10:00 am- 11:00 am	Team Meeting
11:00 am - 11:30 am	Consolidate meeting notes, revamp schedule
11:30 am-11:45 am	Productive Meditation while walking to lunch
12:00 pm-1:00 pm	Lunch & phone/social media check-in
1:00 pm-2:00pm	Deep work: crafting client proposal
2:00 pm-3:00 pm	Email
3:00 pm-4:00 pm	Catch-up tasks, requirements, non-urgent to-do list

In determining what limits one needs, the key point is being honest about how they use their devices and technology and their goals for productivity. Breaking technology habits, or even addictions, is not easy, and determining needed limits is only one step in becoming more productive, avoiding burnout, and dodging decision fatigue. Some people need accountability to help them stick to their goals and the limits they set for themselves.

Environmental Distractions

As discussed earlier, a person's workspace can be a major distraction. It can even play a role in mental health and well-being. Clutter often reflects a person's inner mind and the disorganization of their thoughts and lives. [1]

Looking at the cluttered space around them increases stress levels and anxiety about external and internal struggles they may be facing. [2] It can trigger hopelessness and lead to depression, procrastination, and even loss of passion or motivation for the projects on to-do lists. External distractions can be eliminated with a few simple changes, that will allow someone to notice the benefits of an organized space.

When people spend a significant amount of time in one place, they experience "habituation," meaning they become blind to their external environment. This means they may not be conscious of the visual mess, the smells, or the lighting. Unconsciously, however, these aspects of one's environment bomb their senses, and their hormones (cortisol and dopamine) respond to them. The first step in tackling external environmental distractions is to take a step back from the space and look at it with fresh eyes. People need to think about their senses of sight, sound, smell, and touch to determine how to create a space that calms and energizes rather than produces stress, anxiety, and procrastination.

If there are too many objects in the space, one must clear them out. Less visual distractions result in a more serene environment by ridding the room of unnecessary clutter. Sometimes people struggle to let go of their things, so asking what purpose the item serves can help someone clear a room relatively quickly. If the item has no purpose for the tasks the room is designed for, it doesn't need to be there. For example, if a stack of novels is sitting on a shelf in an accountant's office, they have no purpose in that space; the accountant does not need novels to accomplish their job.

This task may feel overwhelming depending on the number of excess objects in the room, and it is okay to feel this way. To combat the stress connected to decluttering, break the task into manageable time chunks. Perhaps 15 minutes a day is all a person can handle. In addition, it is important not to criticize oneself for the clutter or the size of the mess. Simply focus on a small area for a limited time. After the time is up, look at the small space and celebrate the progress made in that small space. Of course, someone may want to keep a few family photos or sentimental things that remind them why they do their jobs or make them smile as they work, but too many of nonpurposeful items become clutter and detract from a calming, distraction-free space.

Once unnecessary items have been removed from the workspace, one can organize to make it easier to keep clean and to optimize the space for productivity. How a workspace is organized will depend on the person and the work being done in the room. Some may prefer a drawer system to keep their work and supplies organized, while others might use a shelving system or filing cabinets. Each person has to find what works best for them and then stick to the system so that they don't have to spend time cleaning up multiple times a week.

After cleaning up the visual clutter and organizing the space, more subtle visual distractions become noticeable.

Specifically, one might notice the lighting in the room is too bright or too low. Light is essential to mental health and physical well-being. A lack of light or an excess of light, can increase stress and anxiety, contributing to more severe mental health issues stemming from damage to hormone-producing areas of the brain. Depression, mental health in general, and productivity are closely linked to low levels of light and bad quality of lighting. [3] Light is measured in color temperature. Ideal lighting is sunlight and light that is of the same color temperature as sunlight. Rooms with enough sunlight, or lighting that has the same color temperature as sunlight, result in greater efficiency, less fatigue, and a better sense of well-being.

Bad lighting quality is either not enough light or artificial light that measures much higher or lower in color temperature than the sun. This bad lighting results in visual fatigue that decreases productivity and impacts circadian rhythms. [4], [5] Both of these effects impact mental health, levels of fatigue, and the ability to focus. Instead of bright fluorescent lights, use natural light from windows, skylights, or doors. If natural light is unavailable, find lamps and bulbs that mimic natural light. Try using a happy light to help regulate circadian rhythm and provide the same benefits as natural light. Be sure to pay attention to the quality of light outside, and when dusk begins to settle, turn down the light in the workspace to mimic what is happening outside and prepare for sleep.

Colors are also an essential part of the visual design of a room. Calming colors that mimic nature, like soft greens and browns, create a relaxing atmosphere that will not subconsciously distract from work. Bright colors, on the other hand, can lead to increased stress levels and add to the problem of distraction and anxiety, leading to procrastination. [6] Views of nature are also important to providing a restful space that allows calm. Taking time to look at nature is not only relaxing but also healing. Hospital patients are often given rooms with views of nature and heal more quickly than those without views. Taking a few moments in the day to look at nature will work to improve mood, repress anxiety, and manage stress levels. A natural view can also help with grounding techniques used to rest the brain and allow it to reset between high-level tasks. If there is no view that showcases nature, hanging a calming painting or photographs of nature can have a similar effect. Similarly, bringing live plants into space is another way to bring nature into a room.

Once the visual cleaning is accomplished, it can be easier to recognize the other senses being assaulted in the room. Someone might begin to notice the smells and sounds of the room. It might smell a little unpleasant if the room has been neglected for a long time. Giving the walls a quick wipe down, dusting the few items left in the room, and vacuuming the floor can make a big difference to the smell of a room. A change in smell might even be noticeable after removing the clutter, as dust has fewer places to settle. Once the room is clean, it might be helpful to gently encourage a specific feeling by diffusing an essential oil blend. Many essential oil blends help relax or increase productivity through smell. Traditionally, lavender has been used to reduce anxiety and promote a sense of calm. There are also oil blends available in pharmacies that use various oils to help achieve a sense of calm. Similarly, there are essential oil blends that promote productivity and focus by blending things like peppermint, basil, or citrus oils. Having a small collection of essential oils ready to diffuse is a great tool to have on hand that can help reduce internal distractions.

Once the mess is gone, someone might notice the noise in the room. With the technology required for jobs, there might be computer fans or electronics buzzing. Sounds from outside of the space might filter their way into the room. For example, construction noises from nearby building sites or traffic from the street outside might penetrate the walls or pour into the room through open windows. These are sounds one might not be able to get rid of, but they can be minimized or countered. A particular genre of music can block these noises and help some concentrate on their work. White noise can help block distracting noises, too. Many apps create music or playlists to help with these issues specifically. Brain.fm is an effective app for music and sounds to help focus, relax, meditate, or even sleep. Brain.fm uses sounds to stimulate the brain to support sustained states, applying various aspects of neuroscience to develop each track. [7] For example, if one chooses music to help with focus, the gentle rhythm promotes long-term, undisturbed attention.

Their dedication to multiple ways to engage the brain moves them beyond many other apps or playlists, although many others have fantastic playlists to help with the problem of noise. Similarly, nature sounds can be effective and provide a sense of the natural world in an otherwise indoor setting. [8]

The last sense to consider is touch. It may feel strange to include when creating a space for work, but it is imperative. Ergonomics are incorporated as part of touch. How do hands, fingers, and wrists feel when someone types? What about how a chair feels? Is it supportive and comfortable? These things help prevent physical pain that can be distracting and damaging over time. In addition to ergonomics, people must consider what makes them feel comfortable. If the office chair is ergonomically correct but feels too cold against a person's back, they must find a way to make it more comfortable. Using a soft throw blanket over the back of the chair can help keep them warm and make them feel good as they sit against it. Similarly, placing soft throw pillows on an office couch feels more inviting as someone enters the room, relaxing them because they feel good about spending time there. [9] If the room is too cold in general, that must be addressed to ensure it does not become a distraction. This may mean adjusting the thermostat or ensuring there is a warm sweater to wear throughout the day. Each problem someone feels can become a distraction, so they must find a solution to solve it, even if it might not be ideal. The materials used to complete work are also important. For example, how does a pen feel? Is it comfortable to hold, too heavy, thick, or difficult to drag across the page? These details can make creating a comfortable space feel formidable, so only do a little at a time. Prioritize by decluttering. The details can come later, over time, as the practice becomes a habit.

Internal Distractions

Just as there are solutions for external distractions, there are solutions for the numerous internal distractions people face. Whether someone suffers from diagnosed mental health challenges or not, everyone struggles with different forms of internal distractions. Even distractions that don't seem severe can greatly impact how someone works, views themselves, and functions in their daily lives. For these reasons, it is important to eliminate these distractions as much as possible. Unfortunately, internal distractions often take more work to diminish than external distractions. Internal distractions reflect personal struggles, and people have often developed habits as a result. These habits are difficult to break and take significant time and effort to change.

Procrastination

One of the most common habits people struggle with is procrastination. [10] There are tactics to break this habit, but the first step is to realize exactly why procrastination occurs. [11] People put things off for many reasons, and the strategy one chooses to break this habit ultimately depends on personal reasoning.

Someone might procrastinate because they might think they are more productive when they are motivated to complete a task; they feel they need the stress of a looming deadline to be productive As a result, they wait for the right moment. If this is the case, they need to shift their perspective about productivity. Unfortunately, if someone isn't motivated to do something in the moment, they likely won't ever be motivated to do it; it will sit on their to-do list forever, weighing heavily as another task that never gets completed. [12]

When someone believes that they work better under pressure, they might wait until the last minute to do something, hoping to produce better work. These people often underestimate the time they need to complete a task to the best of their ability, and the work they produce is rushed and unpolished. Or they are so exhausted by the end of the project that they aren't able to complete the next task, so they repeat this process. This cycle does not assist in avoiding burnout or decision fatigue. Many people spend their time doing multiple little tasks that require many decisions and are ultimately unproductive and have nothing to do with their passions or career goals instead of taking time on the bigger, more significant projects. [13] If someone finds themselves in this cycle, it is time to change their mindset about how they work.

Instead of waiting until the last minute or a moment of inspiration arrives, they simply need to start. They can craft a schedule for each project, breaking it down into smaller parts with due dates for each aspect. Starting with the simplest task within a larger project can be beneficial and provide enough motivation to keep working. If someone needs accountability, they can ask a colleague to help them with the due dates by meeting to discuss their progress. [14] Accountability like this will help mimic the pressure they feel they need while ensuring high-quality work by not having to rush. Once this schedule is in place, they can schedule each day by chunking their time. For example, for two hours each day, they can work on one project, and for another hour, they can focus on a different project or task. Then, they can return to the first project and work for another chunk of time. If they follow this schedule, they will not have to work under real pressure, and they can ensure they stay focused while giving themselves rest from one task by completing something entirely different.

If someone isn't feeling inspired to complete a project or task, it might help to get it out of the way by doing the worst parts first. In doing the part they least look forward to, they won't have it hanging over their heads, and they will be less likely to continue to put the rest of the project off. When the worst is over, the following parts won't be as difficult or tedious. It usually follows that the rest will follow once someone starts something and gets into a flow of work and thought. This means that once someone begins the task they aren't looking forward to, they will find a flow and the work will naturally continue.

It can help to set a timer for ten or fifteen minutes; when that timer goes off, the idea is that a flow of work has already been reached and the work won't stop; they simply need the encouragement of a short period to begin. Once the worst of the tasks are done, rewards for completing them can be helpful. The reward can be something as simple as a piece of chocolate or an activity that brings pleasure or joy. If there is a reward at the end of a task's completion, many people are more likely to get it done to experience the reward. [15]

Each of the strategies discusses can help change the way someone views their to-do list. Instead of perceiving them as overwhelming, discouraging, or uninteresting, they can begin to view them as part of the pathway to success at work. They become a step toward something greater than the task itself. They will feel more accomplished and hopeful as they see productivity results through tasks crossed off their lists of things to do. With a change in attitude toward what they usually procrastinate and a little self-control to manage distractions, people can achieve their goals, become more productive and efficient, and feel more hopeful about their lives.

Perfectionism

When someone procrastinates because of their negative mindset about the tasks on their to-do lists, those attitudes can bleed into how they respond to situations at work and how they approach the work. Emotions are connected to perceptions, so if someone struggles with fear about a particular situation, they can easily fall prey to the belief that they cannot produce the quality of work they want or that others want from them. [16] This belief can spiral out of control and become a self-fulfilling prophecy. Changing attitudes and perceptions about work can help people escape the fog of overthinking, distraction, perfectionism, and the resulting procrastination.

Just as with a habit of procrastination, a mindset used to the pressures of perfectionism takes patience, work, and self-compassion to change. One of the biggest things to consider when someone suffers from a need for perfectionism is that they are human; this means they have strengths and limitations. [17] No matter how hard someone tries, they cannot always be absolutely perfect. They must let go of some things, realizing that not every problem can be fixed. [18] Sometimes this is because the problem isn't theirs to solve, there is no solution, or the problem doesn't need to be fixed.

It can be easier to recognize this fact when one steps back from the situation they find themselves in. If they can imagine a stranger in the situation, they can more easily disentangle from the situation and see it from a realistic point of view. They can imagine themselves listening to a stranger telling them the details of the situation, and they can more easily sift the important from the unimportant. It then becomes essential not to criticize oneself for overthinking or obsessing over unimportant details. These thoughts are unproductive and tend to lead people deeper into perfectionist tendencies, inevitably leading to more stress, anxiety, and procrastination as they distract from important things. Simply assess the reality of the situation, breathe, and move forward.

Moving forward isn't always easy, so focused attention meditation can help someone refocus while clearing the mind and refreshing them. When a person has cleared their mind of negative self-talk and criticism, they can create a strategy for moving past the problem by focusing on the final result. Setting clear goals for the outcome of each project provides something to work toward and keeps people accountable for what is important in the long run. When someone finds themselves spiraling, they can go back to their vision and ask if the problem they are currently facing will impact the project's outcome. If the answer is no, they can refocus with no worries. If yes, they can focus on a plan to address the problem and continue moving forward.

Stress Management

Sometimes, internal distractions related to perfectionist pressures feel out of control, and it is too difficult to step back from the situation. In these cases, people must apply other strategies to ensure they can eventually step outside the tornado of overthinking, self-doubt, and negative self-talk.

There are many methods to relieve some of the stressors that plague people, but sometimes something quick that doesn't require a massive life change is needed. In these cases, "the four A's of stress relief" can help people relax in moments of intense stress and eventually avoid it altogether. This strategy applies four words beginning with the letter "a": avoid, alter, accept, and adapt. [19]

These four words are simple to remember and, when applied, remind people what is important in the moment.

The word "avoid" implies that someone goes out of their way to keep away from something they find stressful. People cannot always accomplish this, but they can avoid some stressors sometimes. This is different than procrastination. Instead, it means one is physically removing themselves from a stressful situation. For example, if their boss asks them to take on a new project when they already have too much to do, they can avoid the stress by saying "no" or asking for one task of equal value to be removed from their plate. In this way, they avoid the stress of an added project. Similarly, if they find being around someone stressful, they can avoid them by leaving when they come near, closing an office door to avoid them walking into the office, or simply reducing the time spent with them.

"Alter" suggests clear communication with others to change the way they normally interact. For example, if someone often comes to the office, leans against the doorframe, and spends thirty minutes ranting about their team members, this situation can be altered by clearly stating that they only have two minutes because another task is waiting completion. A clear guideline helps set expectations with others and gives an out when needed. This method doesn't immediately shut the person down and make them feel less valued because they are allowed to vent, but not on their timeline.

"Accept" allows people to give up control when avoiding or altering can't be accomplished. If someone can't accept a situation, they end up ruminating about it, increasing their stress levels and anxiety, eventually leading to other internal distractions and reduced well-being. Taking a breath and telling oneself they cannot do anything about this, but the moment will pass helps with acceptance of a situation. If the stressful situation results from one's actions, self-forgiveness is essential in moving forward. Offering oneself compassion prevents becoming stuck in the situation.

Lastly, "adapt" requires a change in expectations of oneself and their situations. People often put more stress on themselves by bundling expectations of perfection that become unrealistic. It might seem like a great plan to have balanced meals three times a day, every day, with no take-out. This could be a realistic expectation if someone never had to work long hours. However, when this desire is bundled with the expectation that they will perform every task at work with absolute excellence, the standards become unrealistic. Instead of aiming for perfection in every area, "adapt" forces people to look at what is reasonable to expect from themselves and make that their reality. This immediately reduces stress as they no longer feel they can't attain the goals they set. People must also focus on the positive in their lives, looking at what they have accomplished rather than what they have not. Celebrating accomplishments helps prevent falling into the hopelessness and depression that comes with feeling overwhelmed by all that is yet to complete. [20]

Remembering to apply these four words on a daily basis can help immensely reduce stress. If someone takes a moment at the end of each day to assess their stressors and how they can apply the four A's for the next day, they will notice a difference in how they approach their lives, themselves, and their jobs. They won't find themselves replaying each stressful scenario because they are making a plan of action instead of obsessing. They may even notice a difference in how others approach and treat them.

Grounding Techniques

Often, when people feel stress and anxiety rising, emotions are difficult to control. They can take over, and everything someone knows they are supposed to do flies out the window. They find themselves heated, defensive, and even yelling. This often escalates the situation they find themselves in, increasing the stress and anxiety. In these situations, people must quickly gain control of their emotions. This will help reduce stress and internal distractions and help preserve energy stores by regulating emotions quickly and effectively. Quick and easy grounding techniques are the best way to regain control of emotions. Grounding techniques rapidly bring people focused attention without needing a quiet space to meditate. Anyone can do them in meetings without others in the room even noticing.

One of the most common grounding techniques is the 5, 4, 3, 2, 1 strategy. This simple strategy can be done silently and quickly, bringing people into their present and distracting them from a stressor long enough to reset their brains and emotions. This technique requires one to breathe and use the five senses, allowing them to fully engage with their present and become mindful of the moment rather than the stress. [21]

First, they breathe, long and slow. Then they notice and acknowledge five things they can see around them. The objects acknowledged don't have to be specific; they can be any size, color, or category. The purpose is to take the mind off whatever escalates emotions, stress, or anxiety and focus it on something else. After identifying five things seen, they move on to four things they can touch. These things might be part of their body or be directly in the space around them, like the chair they sit in, the desk in front of them, or the keyboard they type on. As with the things seen they do not have to be specific or fit into a particular category. They simply need to be things they can physically feel with their body.

Three things a person can hear is the next stage of this grounding technique. The sounds acknowledged should originate outside of the body. External noises help move the focus away from oneself and their emotions better than thinking about whether or not an elevated heartbeat is audible. After recognizing the traffic outside, the birds chirping in the trees, or the hum of a computer fan, they focus on two things they can smell. Since smells may be harder to identify, whatever a person can smell is fine. It might be the smell of carpet warmed by the sun or the warm ink in the photocopier. It might even be the smell of the garbage in a bin somewhere. Be prepared to acknowledge unappealing odors since there may not be much choice about where this technique must be used.

Lastly, identify one thing that can be tasted. This can be anything from the food in the next meal to the tea in a mug on the desk or even the taste of the air, if necessary. The thing identified doesn't actually have to be tasted; its existence and the fact that it can be tasted just needs to be acknowledged. With the progression of each of these steps, it is important to breathe deeply. After the last step, one can take a deep breath and let it out slowly before returning to view whatever elevated their emotions in the first place with fresh eyes, some distance, and a clear head.

Another easy grounding technique is simply sitting with one's feet flat on the ground, hands on thighs, and doing some counting breaths. [22] For this technique, a person breathes in through their nose for a count of four, holds their breath for a count of five, and releases their breath through their mouth for a count of six. If they have the time and space, they can notice how it feels to have their feet on the ground and their hands on their thighs. They can even take time to notice the temperature of the air or their heartbeat slowing down. Taking five such breaths, with feet planted firmly and fully on the floor helps remind people to be physically grounded. The breaths they take help them be more present, and counting distracts from any anxious thoughts that may be circling inside their head and ensures they take adequate breaths for their brain to calm down. People can do this strategy quickly and quietly when they feel overwhelmed; often, no one needs to notice they are doing it.

Grounding techniques are helpful tools to bring people back into the present moment when they feel overwhelmed, stressed, anxious, or even hopeless and depressed about their situations. They can be used as band-aids, but they do not solve the root of the problem. To truly get unstuck in life and at work, people must make changes that allow them to be more productive, reduce decision fatigue and help avoid burnout.

Delegating

One of the most effective ways to ensure success in our work is to delegate. Sometimes people believe that no one else can do their job the way they can. This statement has some truth because everyone is different and has unique strengths. The challenge with this belief is that it often extends to the idea that no one else can do as good of a job as they can. This is not true. The whole truth of the first statement is that sometimes others can do the job better.

Perhaps someone struggles to trust that anyone else can do the necessary research about a topic for a project. They know that they can do a great job and end with a thorough understanding of the topic. When someone is stuck in the belief that no one else will do it as well as they will, they fail to consider someone might already have done it better. There are experts who do not need to take the time and effort to research the topic because they already have the knowledge, information, and experience. [23] By delegating this part of a project to an expert, they relieve themselves of the responsibility to research and the burden of making any decisions connected to this part of the task. They also open their calendars, since the time they would have spent researching is cleared from, their calendar. Instead of spending days gleaning information, the same knowledge can be obtained in a matter of hours in a meeting or a phone call.

Delegation of tasks and decisions doesn't always have to be to an expert. Surveys and questionnaires to clients, colleagues, the public, or strangers can all be forms of delegating decisions. Each decision someone else makes means less energy expended from the decision bank. A person who delegates decisions doesn't feel as tired as quickly, and they can be more confident about their choices because they have input from others.

Most often, when faced with a difficult decision, people feel afraid of making the wrong choice. The fear and anxiety connected to the choice being faced add another level of exhaustion as they work to regulate their emotions. In addition, internally, people overview the possible outcomes of the decision and how each outcome will affect them and their emotions. [24] Ultimately, people are looking for the good feeling that comes from a release of dopamine when they feel the reward of making a good decision. People fear the dopamine dip that comes with perceived negative consequences. [25] Delegating decisions avoids this entire biological and emotional roller coaster. Delegating is one of the best ways to reduce decision fatigue and avoid burnout. [26]

Action Steps

Without purposeful limits and strategies, people struggle to align their actions with their priorities and goals. Distractions are simply too prolific. It can also feel overwhelming to apply every strategy to deal with every distraction. Moving forward, choose one of the following suggestions to help you manage your distractions to increase efficiency and productivity.

1. Assess how you use technology and set two limits that will help you to make the most of your time.
2. Assess the space you use for work and remove as many visual distractions as possible. Then slowly work on organizing the space to support your productivity.
3. Look at the most stressful project you are currently working on, and determine what tasks, activities, and decisions can be delegated to someone else.

When any of these strategies are applied, you can experience greater focus and peace within a busy life.

Chapter Summary

- The internal and external distractions faced are not insurmountable when people apply strategies to deal with them.
- Setting limits for technology use will help with productivity and mental health.
- Creating a comfortable space with few distractions helps clear the mind and calms emotions so people can focus.
- Applying strategies to manage stress can allow people to move forward in their jobs and lives.
- Grounding techniques can be used as a quick, band-aid solution for emotional regulation during high stress.
- Delegating is an important strategy for avoiding decision fatigue and ensuring we do not take on more than we can handle.

6

MAKING DECISIONS WITH LESS ENERGY

HOW TO PRIORITIZE AND TACKLE DECISIONS EFFICIENTLY

J ason sighed as he ended the call with his childhood friend. His friend was struggling to get everything done at work, her husband was attending to his parents across the globe, and she needed someone to look after her kids for an afternoon while she caught up on work. Of course, Jason said "yes" to the request. That is what good friends do, but he was tired. Jason felt like he had nothing left to give, and the truth was that he found himself in a similar situation at work; He barely made it through his client lunch the other day, scraping by with the skin of his teeth to get the client to sign the deal. He also had a big meeting to lead at work the next day. He needed some time to rest and recharge to offer his best work on that presentation.

Jason felt like he was always playing catch-up. Not only did he have heavy responsibilities at work, but he wanted to prep healthy meals for his kids for the week. He enjoyed the task and loved turning up the music, letting loose, and creating something deliciously nourishing for the people he loved. It was a way for him to relax and have some fun. He wouldn't be able to do that with his friend's toddler exploring his home. What Jason really needed was someone to look after his kids while he completed tasks that never seemed to get done. Instead, he was piling more on his plate and watching someone else's children.

Jason was afraid of people's reactions if he disagreed with whatever was asked of him. He was terrified he would be deemed lazy or unneeded at work if he didn't say yes to every project and request, ultimately losing his job. And he was valuable at work, but his days were long, and it felt like he never really completed anything without adding two or three more tasks to his list of things to do. Outside of work, he was afraid people would judge him for being selfish, a bad friend, or even a bad parent. When people asked him for something, there was never a multiple-choice answer; the right answer was always "yes." If only there were the option of "no." Even "none of the above" would be better than "yes" all the time.

It can be difficult to determine what is and is not important when the belief prevails that everything asked of someone is essential to their success. There are other options, though. People can choose "no" or "none of the above." In fact, they should choose these options.

When someone is in the habit of spouting affirmative answers when asked to complete something or for a favor, they usually end up with more on their plates than is healthy for them. Even too much of a good thing can be taxing. People get absorbed in everything they must do and forget what is important. As a result, like Jason, they find themselves lagging in their energy and ability to complete tasks. They often end up sacrificing something in their personal lives to meet the expectations set at work. Priorities are often lost amid the chaos, and people struggle to make decisions that matter, often experiencing decision paralysis where they end up with their status quo answer – "yes."

To move forward in life with energy, clarity, purpose, passion, and joy, people must segregate the important from the unimportant and then begin to say "no" to the unessential.

Segregating

When people begin saying no, they find more control and success in their lives. This is not an easy task, however. Society has trained people to do everything under the overarching belief that doing it all and having it all means success. The truth is hidden beneath the shiny appeal of giving our kids every opportunity, earning more money while sitting behind a desk in a bigger office, owning newer cars, and living a glossy social life. It is difficult to sift through the temptation of so many choices and segregate the important from the unimportant. These things do have merit in some instances, but can often end up causing stress and anxiety as people work toward them, exhausting themselves. They think they are in control. They think that saying "yes" will earn that promotion they yearn for. They think they have made a purposeful choice toward a goal. They fail to realize they are suffering from decision paralysis, defaulting to the status quo answer. They are not segregating the important factors from the non-essential ones.

The array of available choices, too, has hampered the ability to make decisions wisely. There are currently more choices available to people than at any other point in history, and humans simply don't have the skills to decide. [1] People don't know how to sift through their choices to determine the best option. In addition to this lack of skills, people are assaulted by almost as many opinions about each choice, each of those opinions made public via multiple media platforms. Before the internet, people could control whose thoughts they were subject to. They might ask their families for help with a decision or their friends. Now, they are often exposed to numerous opinions before they are even offered a choice, making the decision more difficult when it does present itself.

Decisions about life and work are no different, so people must sort through their lists of tasks and requests to determine what is most important; they must segregate. To do so effectively requires exploring, evaluating, and then eliminating. These three steps are the beginning of learning how to make decisions in a world with too many options.

Exploring, Evaluating, & Eliminating

When someone defaults to their standard response, they relinquish control over the situation to someone else. They neglect to take the time to explore the request and evaluate its worth to their success. Failing to explore and evaluate will end in acquiring more than one can and should handle. It will result in failure to contribute in the ways one wants and ultimately with dissatisfaction in one's job and personal life and burnout. [2]

Although it may seem counterintuitive to take the time and energy to explore and evaluate a task before saying yes or no, people ultimately make more time for themselves by doing so and will end up less likely to suffer from decision fatigue. Greg McKeown uses the principles of essentialism to explain that in exploring tasks, people must consider what it will entail, the resources required to complete it, the available resources, how it aligns with their goals, and if it is in alignment with their highest point of contribution. [3]

For example, Jason's friend asked him to spend the afternoon with her kids so she could catch up on work. He ended up feeling overwhelmed and discouraged because he failed to evaluate before giving his answer. Instead of falling back on his standard response, Jason needed to consider the time frame and the energy he would expend looking after the kids. In this case, he was giving up an entire afternoon, sacrificing his ability to prep meals for his family for the coming week. Saying "yes" did not align with Jason's goals to feed his family healthy meals while also relaxing and doing something he enjoys. Since he was unable to rest, saying "yes" did not align with his highest point of contribution to work; he needed time to rest his brain to give his best performance in the meeting the next day. If Jason had taken time to explore the job of watching his friend's children, he could have clearly seen the negative impact on his goals and energy levels. After exploration, evaluation is much easier.

The evaluation stage weighs the value of the task according to one's goals. The purpose of evaluating is to determine if the task at hand is one of the many unimportant tasks that fall onto one's plate or if it is one of the essential few tasks that will contribute to success in their role. In Jason's case, saying yes to his friend did not contribute to his success at work or his goals to provide nutritious meals to his family. People must ask themselves tough questions and commit to providing honest answers to these questions if they want to see a change in how they approach their lives and work. McKeown advocates giving time and energy only to the activities that will allow people to make "the highest possible contribution toward" their goals and their company. [4] This means that people have to determine their greatest strengths within their designated role, and they measure every request that comes their way against that strength and their ability to contribute using it. If they determine that the task does not align with this value, they eliminate it. Jason struggles to say no because he is afraid of people's responses. Asking himself tough questions about the impact of saying yes in this case would mean he would have to face his fear of saying no because in this case, watching his friend's children wasn't his highest point of contribution to his personal or professional goals. He needed to eliminate the task.

The step of elimination is simple: get rid of things. This means going through a task list, and everything that was evaluated to be unimportant to one's goals for the highest contribution can be either delegated to someone else or thrown out entirely. If someone takes the time to pick their top ten priorities, they can weigh each item on their list of things to do against those priorities. Will a task match all of these priorities? Will it allow for the achievement of career goals and company goals by showcasing strengths? If the answer to these questions is yes, it is a task worthy of the to-do list. If not, it can be eliminated. As someone gets better at eliminating, the number of priorities can diminish, allowing them to decide more quickly what to take on and what to let others do. Ultimately, Jason should not have agreed to take his friend's children for the afternoon. The task could have been eliminated before it began had he taken the time to explore and evaluate. As simple as this sounds, it can be one of the hardest things for someone to do.

One of the ways to tackle this difficulty is by breaking down larger tasks or projects into steps that are easier to evaluate. Sometimes when people only see the end product, it is hard to understand the details and steps needed to get there. Without this knowledge, it is almost impossible to accurately evaluate the value of a project toward one's goals. Jason didn't take the time to explore the choice of watching his friend's children, so he couldn't see the details of the job. If he had explored, he would have been able to break the whole job into its independent steps. He wasn't simply letting her kids stay at his house and play with his kids. Jason would have to greet the kids at the door, take the toddler from his friend's arms, and likely soothe them once his friend disappeared. Then he would have to keep the kids and the toddler entertained and distracted, fed, and safe. He might need to take the group of children to the park to expend energy. Each of these tasks takes up more time and energy than simply offering a place for the kids to be while their mom accomplishes work.

At work, leading a meeting that highlights the company's successes to the Board might initially sound like something that propels someone toward their career goals. However, this may not be the case when the project is laid out in steps. If an accountant is asked to do this, but only a small part of the presentation focuses on the company's financial gains, most of the presentation will not require the skills and talents of the accountant. Therefore, it does not align with their highest point of contribution, does not propel them forward in their career, and should be eliminated from a to-do list by either not accepting the job in the first place or being delegated to someone else. The employee may also choose to lead the meeting but divide the presentation between others by delegating sections to people who are experts in each area.

In addition to breaking a project into smaller parts, people must tackle the emotional difficulty of eliminating it. Getting rid of things on a to-do list by not doing them goes against current culture. It can feel like someone is being lazy. Depending on what they eliminate, it can even feel like they are anti-social or selfish. It is important to remember that this step is not about doing fewer things for the sake of doing less; it is not about finally saying "no" to everything. Eliminating is about making time and space to do the things someone is best at even better because they can focus their time and energy on them instead of menial tasks or activities. Eliminating doesn't guarantee someone will spend less time working (although it might); it means they will spend the same amount of time working more effectively. People must understand that they have finite resources of time, energy, and the ability to make decisions. They simply use the energy they would normally use on an unimportant task for an important one. This allows for greater control over one's time, energy, and schedule.

Segregation of tasks, events, and ways people spend their energy may seem daunting in the face of long to-do lists and busy schedules. It takes courage to begin looking honestly at things there may be an attachment to and determining that they are not as important as initially thought. For example, someone might evaluate a project they have been working on for months and determine that it does not belong on their to-do list anymore. This may be difficult to let go of, but it is vital to moving toward the success they want to see in all areas of their life.

It is also not enough to explore, evaluate, and eliminate once. These steps are a long-term ongoing process. If people do not regularly evaluate the tasks and activities they are involved in, they end up piling up again. People find themselves in a cycle of exhaustion, decision fatigue, and the never-ending menial responsibilities others put on their shoulders. Then they need to work through the long to-do lists, reset priorities, and go through the emotional exhaustion of eliminating all over again. Instead of falling into this cycle, people must create systems that help them streamline their work. For example, someone can set an alarm that signals a sort of last call for their workday. They can say that at 3:00 PM each day, they will no longer accept or begin new tasks or projects. Instead, they will consider it the following morning. This allows people to spend the last hour or two of the day doing what they need to do most. It also prevents them from getting caught up in a new task and working late to finish something that came across their desk near the end of the day when they were too tired to evaluate whether or not it aligned with their priorities. People can also talk with their manager about trading their time in a meeting they might not find useful to their highest point of contribution for more time to focus on the jobs that do. In this way, they can potentially cut out unproductive time. This might be difficult for a manager to accept, but if someone's results at work succeed, they will be more likely to allow for concessions so employees can be more productive for their team and the company.

Eliminating sounds like an ideal solution to many problems, but prioritizing can be difficult, especially if someone has not taken time to step back, rest, and re-set from the busyness of their lives. To explore, evaluate, and eliminate effectively, people need to plot their intentions for their lives. Without a clear plan and criteria to measure decisions against, people easily fall into patterns that harm their well-being and send them into decision fatigue before they even see it coming.

Plotting & Prioritizing

Prioritizing allows people to recognize what is essential more quickly and create a system that makes each decision easier, draining less of one's energy and ability to make decisions. Prioritizing must be done intentionally; it does not fall into place without effort.

When someone explores and evaluates, they need to consider all the information before deciding to eliminate. Understanding who is involved in every step of the process, what the end goal is, when there is time for it, when the completion is expected, and where it fits into one's goals and strengths is key to determining whether it should be eliminated. When these things are clear, they can be measured against criteria that will protect the ability to prioritize things that matter. Someone cannot begin to prioritize if they are not clear on their values and how they want to achieve those values.

Values are important to who people are, and they traverse work and personal lives. They are principles people want to live by, and can keep people focused on what matters most. As a result, people must identify what they are. [5] This process needs to be honest and varies from person to person. To live a truly satisfying life, people need to identify what they value rather than what they feel they should value. For example, there is pressure to value a busy social life; but the reality is that someone might value downtime more. It is important to be honest about values so one can truly feel they are living the life they want and achieve their goals. Values also change throughout life, so people need to revisit their values regularly. In Jason's case, he felt he should value helping friends in need. However, when he did, he felt exhausted and hopeless; the truth was that he valued rest and taking care of his family more. He felt deflated that he wasn't able to put tasks that aligned with those values ahead of helping his friend.

Once someone has established what values are the most important to them, every choice that comes their way can be measured against those values in addition to the other criteria set. This makes elimination much easier as fewer tasks will meet all the criteria. It also helps clarify one's chosen purpose, and with clarity comes freedom, energy, and motivation. If Jason had criteria aligning with his values to help him make decisions, he would not have immediately said yes to his friend, and he would have been able to accomplish his goals. By creating these criteria, decisions are made for people, and they don't have to put in the effort to think about them.

In addition to intentionally plotting benchmarks for determining whether to say yes or no to a project, it is also important to plot out final goals. Without doing this, people can fall into the pattern of continuing to work harder and harder rather than accepting that something has been achieved. It is common to be working on a project and believe that there is more to do, more detail to add, something to edit to improve it, or something that will make a product more appealing. Simply understanding the end goal can help avoid that never-ending work. If the end goal can be achieved with what is already done, the project is finished successfully. People see more success in their work when they have an end goal and are consequently motivated to continue. They can feel meaningful again rather than fall into the hopelessness of never achieving anything worthwhile.

Schedules & Rituals

Another way to use less energy in making decisions and keep to-do lists shorter is to schedule activities and time. If these schedules are crafted based on personal values and priorities, they become meaningful rituals that provide a sense of control. This is particularly important because there are many things people cannot control that throw a wrench into their day, weeks, and sometimes even their lives. [6] Following rituals guarantees people control what they can rather than letting others set their priorities. [7]

These rituals also make decisions for people, reducing the time spent thinking about what to do next and the energy it takes to make decisions. [8] When someone spends less energy on these decisions, they can avoid decision fatigue, save their energy, and focus on decisions that are more important and often more difficult to make. Creating an end-of-day ritual means someone never needs to decide what time to stop working and what tasks to do before the end of the day. If their ritual is to begin a shutdown process at 4:00 PM every day, they no longer need to think about what time they need to be done work. When the tasks inside that ritual conclude the work for the day and set up the work for the next day, they no longer need to decide on the go about which tasks need to be finished or what they can do before they leave the office. It is all set for them every day.

Of course, there needs to be some flexibility in the ritual, but not much. For example, if someone has an appointment at 3:00 PM one day, they can adjust the ritual time, not the ritual. If the process takes an hour, they must start at 2:00 PM instead. Again, this decision has already been delegated to the shutdown ritual and is not one they are making that day. These first choices can be difficult because they break old habits and go against the belief that working harder and longer means success. [9]

Remembering priorities is helpful when making this first decision to avoid future ones. Applying the principle of increasing the importance of a task can help too. [10] This principle suggests that the task one must do instead of making the same decision repeatedly must be more important than that repeated decision. Someone might decide, for example, that taking care of the dog with a long walk every afternoon at 5:00 PM is more important than staying at work to finish a few extra tasks. This particular example might be easier to implement because if the dog doesn't get a long walk, there may be a mess to clean up, or the energy it needs to expend comes out in all the wrong behavior. When someone considers the possible consequences of not leaving to walk the dog, it becomes more important to leave work at a designated time. If someone doesn't have a pet to walk, picking children up from daycare, or even cooking and eating a healthy meal for dinner, can be their motivating factor. As someone becomes used to creating rituals that allow them to control their time and make fewer decisions, reserving their energy and taking less from their decision-making reservoir, they will need fewer motivators. Their values and priorities will become clearer, and finding ways to automate decisions will be more natural. [11]

A shutdown ritual is not the only way to make a single decision that will morph into multiple future decisions. Many areas of life have room to incorporate decisions that will multiply. Amazon's feature of subscribing is a great example of this. This feature allows customers to set designated delivery times for items they buy repeatedly.

They can set the frequency of delivery once and never have to think about it again. They will never have to expend energy deciding whether or not they have enough toothpaste, so they don't have to decide about putting it on the grocery list. They never have to stand in an aisle at the drugstore or grocery store faced with five different brands of toothpaste and ten different kinds of toothpaste in each brand and think about which one they should choose this time. The decision has already been made in their Amazon subscription. There are meal delivery services that can do the same thing for people, cutting down on the number of decisions made about food both in meal planning and at the grocery stores. People can have automatic withdrawals from their bank accounts to pay bills, save for the future, or help budget how they spend money.

People can also begin their day with rituals. One of the most common automated decisions is setting the alarm to help wake up at a certain time. This decision can easily be extended into a ritual that sets someone up for their desired day. For example, someone might set their alarm a little earlier each day. When the alarm goes off, they get up, do some productive meditation while they shower, make a cup of coffee or tea, and then head to a quiet space to accomplish two hours of deep work before their phones and e-mails begin notifying them of everyone else's work crossing into theirs. Similarly, someone might find that beginning their day with focused attention meditation helps set them up for the day. Creating a ritual around this activity will ensure that every day the decision about what time to wake up and how to accomplish everything in the morning is already made. Some people find it helpful to schedule each day, chunking their time to help them stay focused and avoid deciding what to do and when. They simply follow the schedule. [12]

Other people have even taken decision fatigue avoidance through one-time decisions into the details of their lives. People have pre-decided breakfasts or only a single brand and type of coffee, so they never have to choose what to eat or drink first thing in the day, saving their energy resources for bigger decisions throughout the day. Some people have paired their closest down to essentials and only a few colors to save their decision-making resources for bigger decisions later in the day. The one-time decisions someone makes will depend on where they want to expend their energy and where they want to save it. Some people enjoy picking the perfect outfit from a closet full of colors, styles, and fabrics. The key is determining where they are expending their decisions unnecessarily and where they can cut back on making them. Having each of these decisions made provides peace of mind that removes much of the clutter and overthinking that accompanies decision fatigue.

In addition, these choices delegated to scheduled rituals provide momentum in people's lives; they move people forward because they do not end up stuck in decision paralysis or making decisions with the lack of inhibition associated with decision fatigue. [13] & [14] People aren't left cleaning up a mess they made by making an unwise choice or trying to figure out why they made it in the first place. People are less distracted and more able to focus on the things they want to prioritize. They spend less time procrastinating because of internal distractions and less time on external distractions because the rituals are purposeful and meaningful. People enjoy them, find purpose in them, and feel accomplished following them. These rituals make it easier to distinguish work and personal life, providing a work-life balance that is otherwise almost impossible to achieve. They set people up for a life of purpose, success, and fulfillment.

Action Steps

Understanding that there is always a multiple-choice answer when asked to take on something new offers freedom in a feeling of relief. There is another way, even if it contradicts how people normally operate.

Take a moment to write out your top three strengths. Then look at the first three tasks on your to-do list. Explore each task by breaking it down into smaller steps. Evaluate whether or not these tasks align with your highest point of contribution. Are there any tasks or steps you can delegate or toss out entirely?

Next, plot your end goals for each remaining task. What is the purpose of the project, and what will it look like when it meets that purpose? When the project meets that purpose, recognize it as complete. Then you can benefit from a sense of accomplishment that increases confidence in competency and provides motivation for the next step.

As you see success in these areas, work a ritual into your day that solidifies these processes so they become habits that lead to success and decrease the need for making numerous decisions. Unlike Jason, you don't have to find yourself exhausted and unable to make choices that drain your energy resources.

Chapter Summary

- Just because "yes" is the expected answer doesn't mean it is the only answer; people can and should say no when something doesn't align with their values and goals.
- Exploring and evaluating choices, proposed projects, and suggested activities helps people determine what to eliminate, say no to, and delegate.
- People can automate decisions so they only have to make them once and can reap the benefits of future decisions already being made.
- People must plot their goals and intentions to manage stress and ensure they understand when they have reached the end of a project or activity.

7

MAKING PURPOSEFUL DECISIONS

HOW REMOVING DECISION FATIGUE CAN LEAD TO A LIFE OF CLARITY, CONTROL, AND MEANING

Michelle's experience with an intense rest period moved her career and life forward in ways she never imagined possible while she was slouching on her couch eating chips for dinner. She was excited about her work, and she divided her time between work and home carefully to ensure she created work-life balance for herself. With the extra time and energy she had, she dove into learning how to become more efficient and productive.

As a result, Michelle integrated a morning routine into her day, beginning with a 10-minute meditation. Her focus increased, and she had an easier time keeping her values and goals top of her mind. She even learned how to gently let her boss know when she wasn't the right person for a project. Her boss respected her ability to prioritize and even suggest a different person for the project, never questioning her opinion. She had autonomy in her projects, providing satisfaction she never expected she could have.

There were times when her to-do list felt overwhelming, and work took up more time than she would like, but she knew how to balance those times with purposeful rest instead of slumping in front of the television. She also knew how to delegate some of the tasks on those ever-growing lists to shorten them. The number of days when tasks were overwhelming was significantly less than days that felt not only manageable but enjoyable.

Michelle was even able to take time to repair her relationship with her traveling friend in addition to spending more time with her other friends and family. She felt fulfilled knowing what was important and how to achieve it.

Michelle is not the only person who can experience a life of clarity, control, and purpose leading to empowerment. When people embrace the knowledge that they have limited resources, can't do it all, and that this is okay, they can begin to see change in their lives. They can begin to find paths toward the life they desire, paths to real success rather than perceived success.

The Benefits Of Knowledge

Confucius stated long ago that "education breeds confidence. Confidence breeds hope. Hope breeds peace." [1] The passage of time and the current society doesn't diminish the significance of this quotation. In fact, it enhances it. People are surrounded by more information than they know what to do with, some of it untrue. The key to experiencing the truth of this quotation is finding the right information for the problems people face rather than all the information on as many topics as they possibly can. People need to be educated about the things that impact them directly. Learning about the existence of decision fatigue can offer significant relief. There is nothing wrong with anyone who feels overwhelmed. No one is stupid for not having all the answers. No one is incapable or lazy just because they can't get it all done–people are simply burned out in the midst of a society that promotes unhealthy habits.

When people understand that their bodies and brains have limited capacity, and withdrawals of precious resources happen more often than is good for them, they can breathe again. This scientific fact gives people freedom from society's pressures. This knowledge also provides solutions to the problem of decision fatigue leading to burnout and the diminished well-being people feel as a result.

With solutions, people can move forward in the direction they want to go with clarity. They don't feel lost in the middle of other people's priorities, beliefs, and hopes for life. With knowledge, people know what their brains and bodies need to be healthy and well, and when they apply this knowledge in ways that work for their lives, values, and priorities, they see results. They begin to experience things they have not experienced in the way they view the world around them and how others view and treat them. They may even get to do activities they have only dreamed of having the time and energy for. With this newfound clarity, people can more easily make decisions that lead to true success rather than falling back to the status quo of agreeing to something they don't really want to do, can't do well, or procrastination. They no longer find themselves doing only tasks and activities that drain their resources or don't find meaningful.

The clarity that comes from being educated in the things that matter to someone puts the control back in their hands. Understanding that they can delegate offers more time where before there was no time. Knowing that delegation of tasks and decisions is not about passing the work off to someone else, but about letting everyone's strengths shine alleviates the guilt associated with not being as busy. Delegation done correctly leads each person involved in the process into their own space of highest contribution, ultimately benefiting everyone more than simply accomplishing the task to a mediocre standard. The time people get back from delegating decisions and tasks means they can spend that time on meaningful projects rather than on tasks they feel they must accomplish to get caught up or appear successful and valuable. That sense of control moves beyond providing time, to finding meaning within one's job and life, and protecting people from burnout. [2]

When someone is not expending energy making excess decisions, regulating emotions, and displaying self-control, they can use that energy in activities and projects they know will give them purpose in and outside of work. People can feel confident their strengths are being used as they complete work that grows their skills, contributes to the company, and makes a difference with creativity and innovation. There is purpose in people's days when they are clear on how their work will influence the world in which they work and live. With this knowledge, they avoid feeling overwhelmed, hopeless, and purposeless as often. These emotions may still rear their heads every now and then, as they did with Michelle, but with knowledge, people can recognize them for what they are, apply strategies, and move forward.

When people aren't stuck in the mire of mental health issues, procrastination, perfectionism, and distraction, they may even have time to volunteer their time outside of work to contribute to the community. They will have time for their families and friends because they can prioritize them with clarity backed by knowledge of the importance of work-life boundaries. With this clarity, control, and renewed purpose, people can truly feel that they are living a meaningful life.

Using Deep Work To Counter Finite Resources

It can be difficult to digest the fact that time and energy are limited resources. When someone thinks about all the people and activities that are draining those resources, it can feel like they will run out before anyone accomplishes the things they want to for themselves. Maximizing these limited resources won't extend the time someone has beyond twenty-four hours in a day, but it can provide more time within those twenty-four hours. It can also help people retain energy stores for activities they want to do in their day. In addition to using strategies like delegating, automating decisions, culling to-do lists, and identifying values and priorities, people can use the concepts connected to deep work to help them lead an intentional life that promotes their success in work and life.

Remember that deep work comprises periods of undistracted time spent on a single project. Within this timeframe, a person works diligently, challenging their skills, and exhausting their brains to produce meaningful work that is difficult for anyone else to replicate. [3] Deep work is accomplished through one of four methods, each catering to a different lifestyle and level of ability when it comes to focused attention. The monastic approach can be difficult for most people to achieve, so the bimodal and rhythmic approaches are the easiest to weave deep work into daily practices, especially as someone is learning how to focus for a long period. These approaches are also the most useful in many jobs, allowing people to dedicate their attention and energy to projects that will make a difference and ultimately result in greater success while still engaging with the world around them and completing other jobs that must be done, no matter how menial they feel. [4]

Once someone cultivates the skill of deep concentration, they can move into the journalistic approach, fitting deep work into their days wherever and whenever they can, even if just for 30 or 60 minutes at a time. Being able to accomplish deep work by rapidly entering into intense focus means a person can accomplish a great deal quickly. Not only will they find they produce more, but the knowledge of how deep work can help them and the world around them is powerful.

Most employees in the workforce are used to fragmented focus and multitasking. Their brains have been trained to shift attention from one activity to the next and back again without recovery or rest time. This way of operating has caused damage to people's cognitive function and their ability to accomplish great work. [5] If a person can master deep work and the art of sustained focus, they can set themselves apart from the rest of the workforce, and guarantee their success in an ever-changing workforce. they will be able to quickly learn the new skills required to work with advancing technology and to use that knowledge to generate work that others simply cannot. With this kind of marketability, they won't find themselves stuck in a job they hate doing meaningless work. Instead, they will be contributing to the world, their companies, and their lives in ways they never thought possible. Their efficiency will increase, and their decision fatigue will fade, allowing them to make wise choices for their lives.

Within the context of deep work, it is essential to remember that people still have limited energy resources. Deep work is not meant to be accomplished without rest periods to provide buffer space between intense periods of focus. Rest and recovery must be viewed as an effective strategy in addition to the other strategies for efficiency. Rest will replenish energy stores, help people avoid the decision fatigue they face, and reduce the amount of energy they expend on emotional regulation in the face of things they cannot control. Rest will help people achieve their goals and increase their productivity, leading them into the "effortless state," when coupled with other approaches to work and life.

How To Make It Effortless

In his book, Greg Mckeown describes the "effortless state" as being in a state where one has let go of their emotions and blocked out all the noise so they can focus on "the right things the right way." [6] Entering this effortless state, makes life more manageable and easier to live. This state is experienced when individuals are rested, not bogged down by emotions, energized, aware, alert, attentive, and focused on what is important to them. [7] Getting to the effortless state takes work, but it is not impossible.

Physically Rested

In seasons, nature models the ebb and flow of life needed for growth. Animals hibernate after periods of intense mating, birthing, and foraging. They take the winter to slow down and rest, preparing for the next season of hard work. Historically, humans followed these seasonal patterns, but with the industrial age came the focus on constant flow. [8] There was less need to rest because things that weren't available during winter in previous times were suddenly available and there was nothing to force rest. The importance of rest slowly diminished as the trajectory of life on Earth changed.

Sleep is not given the attention it needs as people work late into the night or socialize until the early hours. These are actions they believe propel them forward, but the reality is they are not operating at their best capacity.

Studies indicate that people who consistently sleep less than 7 hours a night are more likely to suffer serious health issues. Studies indicate that less than 7 hours of sleep a night increases the chances of "cardiovascular disease, heart attack, stroke, asthma, arthritis, depression, and diabetes. [9] If people consistently sleep less than 6 hours a night, they experience cognitive deficits and a decline in motor skills seen in people who miss an entire night of sleep. Without adequate rest, it is impossible for a person to experience the effortless state because work and life not only feel harder, but are more challenging while fighting the physical and mental impacts of fatigue. In addition to these symptoms, there is an overarching mindset that sleep can wait–that people can catch up on sleep when the current project is done. For most people, that day rarely comes as a new project awaits the completion of the old one. They keep pushing through the work, believing that it is the best way to get things done. This is another common fallacy.

If people want to experience the benefits of sleep, they must choose to do so, working it into their schedules. One of the ways to ensure adequate rest is to make sleep into an appointment by putting it into the schedule for the day. Reminders can be set on a digital calendar for a specific time each night. When the alarm goes off, it is time to stop whatever is happening and head to the bedroom for the appointment with sleep. Setting the alarm will help develop the habit of prioritizing sleep. After enough nights of good sleep, a person will be able to see the difference in their productivity as they struggle less to concentrate and come up with solutions to the problems they may be tackling at work or even at home.

However, it isn't always easy to get the recommended 8 hours of sleep at night, even when someone makes sleep appointments a habit. Naps can help make up for the sleep deficit that happens when people sleep less than 6 hours at night. In fact, napping for 90 minutes can result in the same benefits as sleeping 8 hours at night. Depending on a person's schedule during the day and evening, they may find it beneficial to plan for 6 hours of sleep each night and a 90-minute nap at some point in their afternoon. How a person plans their sleep will depend on the responsibilities and activities they have in their life, but making time for sleep must be a priority if they want to meet their potential and achieve their goals.

At other times, people experience more fatigue because of increased stress or emotionally challenging times. During these periods, rest is essential to prevent decision fatigue, burnout, and other mental health issues. Naps are a great way to accomplish this rest. McKeown calls daytime naps, "effortless naps" not because they are easy to take, but because taking naps when one feels tired can help move them into the effortless state. When someone feels like concentration is difficult, it is time to rest. An effortless nap can be the perfect type of rest because it will ensure better cognitive function a few minutes after waking. [10] To take an effortless nap, set an alarm to avoid worrying about oversleeping or waking up on time for an appointment or meeting. Then block out all sound and light using blackout curtains or an eye mask and noise-canceling headphones or earplugs. The last step is not as easy; it requires a person to dispel all thoughts about what they could be doing instead of napping. [11]

Some people might feel guilty about taking a nap in the middle of the day because they might feel they are being lazy, or that others will perceive them as such. The truth is that they will end up doing more in the day by taking a nap for an hour or two than if they push through their exhaustion. The work they produce will be of higher quality and will showcase their skills and talents. They will also accomplish this kind of work much easier and more efficiently because they won't be fighting fatigue and the emotions that are more difficult to regulate as a result.

Whether someone is sleep deprived or not, a nap can help boost their mood and ability to function. [12] Alertness and cognitive function are enhanced considerably when people sleep from anywhere between one and eight hours.

A nap of only a few hours can counter the decline in performance normally seen when people spend long hours at work. [13] This means that when someone begins to feel tired, they will be more productive if they take a nap or get a good night's sleep rather than pushing through. Late nights at the office don't actually become as productive as one might think, and certainly don't allow for optimal performance. People simply cannot reach their potential if they have to force themselves to concentrate because they are tired. [14] Sleep is necessary to finding ease in achieving one's goals, and the best way to be physically rested is to avoid exhaustion in the first place rather than attempting to catch up at a later time.

Unburden Emotionally

The human brain can be compared to a whiteboard. There is a limited amount of space for thoughts and emotions to exist. When the board is full, there is no room for anything new. [15] If a person is holding onto thoughts, ideas, and emotions from the past, there is no room for new ideas, thoughts, or emotions relevant to their present. They are held back from success as a result, and exploring new ideas and seeing forward movement becomes hard work, if not impossible. To get into the effortless state, they need to unburden themselves of emotions that do not serve them.

Often, people carry burdens that are not their responsibility to carry. They empathize with others and then fail to let go of those emotions once the moment for empathy is finished. Others believe they need to feel a particular emotion to satisfy another person. For example, someone may hold onto the feeling of guilt because when they were younger, they accidentally broke someone's leg, preventing them from attending their high school prom. This guilt does not serve them and simply takes up whiteboard space. On the other hand, someone might be holding a grudge against someone who received the promotion they wanted. [16] This anger and resentment take up space and often have residual effects within the workplace. All of these emotions need to be released in order to move forward and make room for new and relevant ideas and emotions to fill the whiteboard. Unfortunately, there is no magic solution to letting go of these emotions, and it can help one's success in this area to work with a professional to release the emotional baggage.

People can also be burdened by old goals, suggestions, or ideas that no longer hold any weight. They fail to recognize that these things are no longer important to them or will no longer work toward their success. [17] As a result, they are still taking up space, making it more difficult to come up with new ideas or innovations. For example, someone may have received the advice of buying an old house, fixing it up, and selling it for a profit, restoring a historic home to its former glory. Thinking this was an appealing suggestion, they tucked it into the back of their mind and focused on their career in analytics consulting. As time progressed, they never let go of the suggestion, returning to it every now and then. Eventually, it made no sense for them to use this as a profit gain. Instead, it would eat up time and resources that could be used to achieve more income through more clients. The idea, though, still takes up space and energy that could be used for other endeavors. Recognizing old ideas that no longer hold the most value for a person allows people to more easily accept other ideas, suggestions, and goals that align with what is essential to their life in the present. In this way, progress becomes effortless and experiencing mental energy is easier.

Becoming Mentally Energized

When someone has freed themselves of unnecessary emotions, they can experience something different than the common state of exhaustion, hopelessness, and negativity. Instead, there is room for gratitude, joy, and positivity. These emotions are solidified when one experiences the results in their work and life. Without anger, frustration, or anxiety bogging someone down, there is more energy for the projects they must complete. There is more energy to look at things from a new perspective, and to ultimately make work and life easier. Simply asking the question, "How can I make this process easier?" allows individuals to see a task in a different light. [18] When this question is coupled with what McKeown calls "10 minute microbursts," new solutions become visible where before it seemed there were none. In a microburst, a person takes 10 minutes to focus intently on a single activity or problem. When that 10 minutes is over, progress in a single area has been made, usually more than one expects. The result is increased motivation and renewed energy to continue working on the problem, if it hasn't already been solved. [19]

Microbursts are also useful to help people pace themselves rather than overwork themselves. Since a microburst is meant to be a time of high-intensity focus, it should be followed with rest, even if just for one minute. [20] Similarly, to avoid exhaustion instead of recovering from it, break periods of work into smaller chunks. McKeown suggests no more than three chunks of work for 90 minutes at a time with a 10 or 15-minute break between work periods. [21] How long a person chooses to spend in each work period is up to them and their ability to focus. If someone has become an expert in focusing, is enjoying the task, and still feeling energized, they may decide to schedule two-hour chunks of time instead of 90 minutes. The important part of chunking periods of focused work is the rest between them. Even people who engage in deep work for extended periods take rest periods after their work. [22]

In addition to pacing work for greater productivity and exploring new ideas, gratitude increases one's energy. When someone focuses on what they have accomplished, they can celebrate with joy, inviting this energizing emotion into their life. [23] Instead of feeling weighed down by what they haven't accomplished and the emotions of guilt, frustration, anger, resentment, or hopelessness connected to that mindset, people can reap the benefits of physical, psychological, and social resources. As someone feels and shows gratitude for the people in their life, their relationships become richer and they experience greater awareness of other people. The same principle applies to the accomplishments they have made and even the things they own. McKeown guarantees his own grateful attitude by following every complaint with a statement of gratefulness. It might feel impossible to avoid complaints when things don't go as expected, but when the kitchen sink begins to leak and someone finds themselves complaining about the wasted water, hiring a plumber, and taking the time to fix it, they can follow those complaints with statements of thanks. For example, they could say they are thankful they have a kitchen sink, or that they have the money to pay a plumber, or that they have running water in a home that shelters them from the elements. In this way, there is a constant return to joy and positivity that washes away the negative and allows one to remain mentally energized. Mental energy also leaves more energy for noticing one's present moment and engaging with it. When a person can do this, relationships, work, life, and prioritizing are easy.

Being Aware Of The Present

Increased awareness of the present moment cannot happen without being emotionally unburdened, physically rested, and mentally energized. Each of these builds on the others to create a life where a person effortlessly achieves the essential things. Previous chapters discuss the benefits of mindfulness meditation to reduce stress and increase cognitive function by carving neural pathways. McKeown takes awareness of the present beyond stress relief and cognitive function to explore the practical benefits of heightened awareness.

When someone is aware of the present, it is easier to sift the relevant from the irrelevant because anything not pertinent to the present moment is not important. [24] It might be important at a later time, but not currently, and so can be ignored. When the unimportant is ignored, it is essentially erased from the whiteboard, leaving room for other things in the present moment to fill the space. Just as on a real whiteboard, when ideas or thoughts are written out, people can start to draw lines connecting them. These connections allow for innovation as understanding is expanded. More awareness of what matters to the present moment means the ability to see things with a laser-sharp focus that otherwise wouldn't exist. [25]

Similarly, being focused on the present means people leave opinions, advice, and judgment out of it since these all stem from the past. This is hard, and it takes practice and conscious effort to exist only in the present moment. It is important, however, because without these lenses, people can see others more clearly. Actions and words stand independently from prejudices. Alertness increases as one must watch carefully to make sense of the truth of the situation rather than letting previous opinions take control. McKeown discusses using this skill to hire the right person for a job. Focus on the present with an open mind forces an interviewer to hear precisely what is being said and done. It forces one to observe rather than simply see, and it forces a person to be present in the moment rather than just a body in the room.

It can be tough getting to this place of complete release resulting in heightened perception and awareness. It helps to be rested and unburdened by emotions and mental exhaustion. It helps to have an attitude of thankfulness. It can also be helpful to take a moment to practice a mindfulness exercise. Completing a short mindfulness exercise will move the brain into the state it needs to be in, firing up neural pathways necessary for the focus. If someone finds that it is still difficult to let go of the muddle of the unimportant, a grounding technique or a focused attention meditation with a mantra for the moment can be helpful.

People may be aware that they are struggling to get to the effortless state McKeown describes, but may feel at a loss as to why. They might find that grounding techniques and meditations aren't helpful long-term, if at all. In these cases, it is important to consider the benefits of seeking professional help to discover the root causes of the emotions they can't seem to get rid of and to walk them through healing from those experiences. Those living with mental health issues may also need more practical support. It can be harder and mean more work initially, but with the right resources, the effortless state is achievable.

Anyone can buy a compass and a map, but if they don't know how to use them, it is easy to get lost. Being in the effortless state is like having a great compass, a good map, and the skills to use them.

Understanding what is important in the present moment means that when thoughts fly unbidden into the brain, one can immediately assess whether they are a feeling or a fact. If there is space on the whiteboard and energy to think, connections can be made that help reveal truth from falsehood or the important from the perceived important. Instead of holding a grudge against someone who got the promotion they wanted, a person can recognize they weren't the best candidate for the job.

In the effortless state, one doesn't have to think about these things anymore; they are simply viewed as second nature. The picture is clear.

Adopting The Right Mindset

Achieving success through these methods is not achieved with a single decision that immediately changes how one lives and operates. It takes hard work and a willingness to learn, to be vulnerable, and to be open to change within oneself. It takes a growth mindset.

Many believe that a growth mindset comes with a positive outlook, flexibility, and open-mindedness. These characteristics, although good traits to have, are not what make up a growth mindset. In her article *What Having a Growth Mindset Actually Means*, Carol Dweck responds to the misinterpretation of the term she coined by underscoring that a growth mindset is about a consistent willingness to learn. [26] It can be easy to spin a moment to the positive, looking for the good in the bad without acknowledging the impact of the bad. It can be easy to offer a little extra time to a colleague who is late submitting a part of their project rather than confront them to ensure more timely results next time. And it can be easy to accept minor changes to accommodate someone else. When people display these characteristics, they think they have been naturally gifted with a growth mindset. Dweck stresses that this is not the case. These characteristics may be the result of having a growth mindset, but do not constitute it.

A growth mindset is an attitude individuals must purposefully pursue. It encompasses the willingness to learn not just through reading books and attending classes, but through mistakes, risk-taking, and being aware of the processes it takes to see results. It means realizing that failure is not the end of the world, but a chance to learn how to move forward. Those with a growth mindset "reward not just effort but learning and progress." [27] People with a growth mindset celebrate seeking help from others, "trying new strategies and capitalizing on setbacks" because they understand that allows them to grow and learn. [28] They know that when they use the expertise of others, they avoid the work of starting from scratch and making the same mistakes others already have. Instead, they can take an idea or knowledge further than they otherwise would have been able to on their own. [29]

People who operate this way experience challenges with excitement because they see them as opportunities to grow rather than as the potential to send them crashing and burning. [30] In order to address the challenges, new information must be gained from various sources, new perspectives explored, and ultimately, their understanding of this aspect of their job or their world will expand. When character flaws or weaknesses surface during this process, instead of beating themselves up, they recognize these moments as exposure to areas for growth, and they reflect on how to move forward from them. They use language that offers compassion rather than judgment. For example, instead of railing at themselves (or others), they encourage viewing the situation as a learning opportunity. In this way, they have an easier time avoiding the need to seek approval from others by creating the image of a perfect employee or a successful professional. The irony is that by adopting the growth mindset, productivity and collaboration increase, which creates the desired image they just don't have to think about it. People with growth mindsets see results in their work and their life. They reach their potential, and become who they want to be easier than those who believe they cannot change themselves.

Despite the benefits of adopting this mindset, it is not a natural way of thinking about the world, and often innate instincts get in the way. When someone faces "challenges, receive[s] criticism, or fare[s] poorly compared with others," the first response is rarely joy at the opportunity to learn. Rather, the first natural responses are disappointment, discouragement, insecurity, and even defensiveness. [31] These emotions aren't wrong, and must be felt, but individuals cannot get stuck there. Instead, they need to pursue a growth mindset, offering themselves compassion along with the reminder that the things they face have the potential to move them forward.

When people stop worrying about what others will think if they make a mistake or take an unusual approach to solving a problem, the exhaustion that accompanies those efforts disappears. Accepting imperfection as part of the learning process allows people to avoid striving for perfection, getting caught in a cycle of procrastination, anxiety, and even hopelessness at ever seeing success (because the target of perfect is never attainable).

Action Steps

With the application of knowledge about the right things comes wisdom. It also brings change to areas where change is needed. Take a moment to reflect on three pieces of information that resonate with you from reading this book. How can this knowledge be applied in your week?

You may find that you learned a strategy that could be useful for reducing stress, or you might find that simply understanding how decision fatigue is impacting your daily life is standing starkly against everything else you read. It doesn't matter what rings true for you, and if three things are too many, begin with one. Michelle's story can be an inspiration. She didn't change everything at once or integrate every single strategy into her life. She applied a few, and she noticed significant results.

You don't have to start quickly either. Find a way to work that knowledge into your life one thing at a time. If it feels like too much to incorporate a daily shutdown ritual like Cal Newport does, try it for Fridays so the weekend is freer. Give yourself permission to take baby steps rather than incorporate everything into your life at once. That will inevitably be overwhelming and discouraging. As time goes on, and you start to see the results of one, two, or three changes, you can start to work more into your daily routines. This, too, is about a growth mindset and allowing yourself time and space to learn.

Chapter Summary

- Knowledge about the right things helps provide a sense of peace while also offering solutions to problems people may not have known existed.
- Deep work creates opportunities in people's lives that ensure their success.
- Being physically rested and free of heavy emotions increases a person's ability to be mentally energized and present, ultimately making success easier.
- A growth mindset allows one to avoid harmful habits and creates a sustainable life that leads people to greater success without as much effort.

AFTERWORD

Jason scoured the cupboards looking for snacks that he could put in his kids' lunches. His friend's toddler had screamed whenever he put her down, and the few hours in the afternoon he initially agreed to had turned into the entire afternoon and evening while his friend ran a few errands on the way to pick up her kids. He barely had time to go to the bathroom, let alone prepare anything for his kids. They had resorted to boxed macaroni and cheese for dinner. The kids loved it, but Jason felt like he barely made it through.

Now, this morning, he was desperately trying to pack his kids something nutritious before hustling them out the door so he could go to the office a little early to get some work done. He sighed, grabbed some apples, pepperoni sticks, lettuce, and granola bars, dividing them into the two lunchboxes on the counter while imagining his kids picking up a leaf of plain lettuce and wondering what they were supposed to do with it. He hoped they would eat it. He also hoped their teachers wouldn't notice his failed attempt at putting together lunches for his kids.

The job summary project his boss had asked him to complete a week ago was due in a few days, and he had barely started it. He hoped that arriving early at the office would give him some time to focus and make some progress. He knew that e-mails piled up over the weekend, though, and by the time he answered those, the office would be bustling. He debated taking a sick day to stay home where it was quiet so he could work undistracted, but he didn't know if that would be the best choice. He couldn't see a way forward for his week, and he felt hopelessness settle in before he was even out the door.

Jason's story highlights the frustrations people experience when they don't understand how decision fatigue and its related side effects impact every area of their life. Jason didn't have strategies to avoid the constant distractions at work, or understand how to achieve deep work to help counter those many distractions. Instead, he found himself caught up in shallow work that he did not find meaningful to his role at work. He was working hard, putting in extra time, but he wasn't getting anywhere. He found himself struggling at work and personally, ultimately ending up frustrated and feeling stuck, struggling to stay afloat and positive.

Michelle's story counters Jason's and reiterates that when someone takes steps to apply strategies, they can move forward, finding success, clarity, purpose, and meaning.

Michelle came to understand that rest was important; it gave her time and space to explore what was important for her and what was essential to her life and career success. With this realization, she made time for it, applying strategies to ensure she prioritized rest. As a result, she could easily see what was and was not important to her role and avoid things that distracted her from those purposeful activities. This process takes work, and sometimes, like Michelle, people must be forced into it. No one has to wait until they experience something extreme to make changes. These changes can be made simply because the knowledge has crossed their path.

When one understands that there are biological limitations to what they accomplish, they can let go of the superhero alter ego that reigns in a world of constant busyness and expectations of perfection. They can work to grow from this knowledge, seeing it as an opportunity to apply a new perspective, new strategies for achieving results, and ultimately a new way of looking at success. They can avoid the great difficulties associated with the old way of approaching work and live within the parameters they set for their own life.

Test the strategies outlined throughout this book and use the knowledge gained to change how you approach work and life. Observe how you feel, how your results increase over time, and even how others respond to you as a result. You will not be disappointed.

YOUR LAST CHANCE FOR OUR LIMITED DEAL

DID YOU LIKE WHAT YOU READ? THEN YOU'RE GOING TO LOVE THE FOLLOWING EXCLUSIVE OFFER...

In general, around 50% of the people who start reading do not finish a book. You are the exception, and we are happy you took the time.

To honor this, we invite you to join our exclusive Wisdom University newsletter. You cannot find this subscription link anywhere else on the web but in our books!

Upon signing up, you'll receive two of our most popular bestselling books, highly acclaimed by readers like yourself. We sell copies of these books daily, but you will receive them as a gift. Additionally, you'll gain access to two transformative short sheets and enjoy complimentary access to all our upcoming e-books, completely free of charge!

This offer and our newsletter are free; you can unsubscribe anytime.

Here's everything you get:

- ✓ How To Train Your Thinking eBook   **($9.99 Value)**
- ✓ The Art Of Game Theory eBook   **($9.99 Value)**
- ✓ Break Your Thinking Patterns Sheet   **($4.99 Value)**
- ✓ Flex Your Wisdom Muscle Sheet   **($4.99 Value)**
- ✓ All our upcoming eBooks   **($199.80* Value)**

Total Value: $229.76

Take me to wisdom-university.net for my free bonuses!

(Or simply scan the code with your camera)

Scan Me

*If you download 20 of our books for free, this would equal a value of 199.80$

THE PEOPLE BEHIND WISDOM UNIVERSITY

Michael Meisner, Founder and CEO

When Michael got into publishing books on Amazon, he found that his favorite topic - the thinking process and its results, is tackled in a much too complex and unengaging way. Thus, he set himself up to make his ideal a reality: books that are informative, entertaining, and can help people achieve success by thinking things through.

This ideal became his passion and profession. He built a team of like-minded people and is in charge of the strategic part and brand orientation, as he continues to improve and extend his business.

Claire M. Umali, Publishing Manager

Crafting books is collaborative work, and keeping everyone on the same page is an essential task. Claire oversees all the stages of this collaboration, from researching to outlining and from writing to editing. In her free time, she writes reviews online and likes to bother her cats.

Brittany Valenzuela, Writer

Brittany is a seasoned teacher of English Language Arts & Literature who has expanded her career to include freelance writing and editing. She writes short fiction and non-fiction books. When she isn't working, she enjoys cooking, biking, camping, or hiking with friends and family.

Andrew Speno, Content Editor

Andrew is a teacher, writer, and editor. He has published two historical nonfiction books for middle-grade readers, a biography of Eddie Rickenbacker and the story of the 1928 Bunion Derby ultra-marathon. He enjoys cooking, attending live theater, and playing the ancient game of go.

Sandra Agarrat, Language Editor

Sandra Wall Agarrat is an experienced freelance academic editor/proofreader, writer, and researcher. Sandra holds graduate degrees in Public Policy and International Relations. Her portfolio of projects includes books, dissertations, theses, scholarly articles, and grant proposals.

Danielle Contessa Tantuico, Researcher

Danielle conducts comprehensive research and develops outlines that are the backbone of Wisdom University's books. She finds pleasure in this role as it allows her to immerse herself in self-improvement topics. An avid reader and a songwriter, Danielle channels her passion for artistic endeavors and personal growth into everything she creates for Wisdom University.

Ralph Escarda, Layout Designer

Ralph's love for books prevails in his artistic preoccupations. He is an avid reader of non-fictional books and an advocate of self-improvement through education. He dedicates his spare time to doing portraits and sports.

REFERENCES

Introduction

1. Wondery. (2021, September 21). Plane crash in the Andes (Season 7, Episode 1). [Audio podcast episode]. In *The crash*. Wondery. https://wondery.com/shows/against-the-odds/episode/8514-plane-crash-in-the-andes-the-crash/

1. Defining Decision Fatigue

1. McKeown, J. (2014). *Essentialism: The disciplined pursuit of less.* Virgin Books.
2. Pignatiello, G. A., Martin, R. J., & Hickman, R. L. (2018). Decision fatigue: A conceptual analysis. *Journal of Health Psychology*, *25*(1), 123–135. https://www.ncbi.nlm.nih.gov/pmc/articles/PMC6119549/pdf/nihms956822.pdf
3. Miserandino, C. (n.d.). The spoon theory. *But You Don't Look Sick.* Retrieved March 16, 2023, from https://butyoudontlooksick.com/articles/written-by-christine/the-spoon-theory/
4. Pignatiello, G. A., Martin, R. J., & Hickman, R. L. (2018). Decision fatigue: A conceptual analysis. *Journal of Health Psychology*, *25*(1), 123–135. https://www.ncbi.nlm.nih.gov/pmc/articles/PMC6119549/pdf/nihms956822.pdf
5. Kishida, K. T., Saez, I., Lohrenz, T., Witcher, M. R., Laxton, A. W., Tatter, S. B., White, J. P., Ellis, T. L., Phillips, P. E. M., & Montague, P. R. (2016). Subsecond dopamine fluctuations in human striatum encode superposed error signals about actual and counterfactual reward. *Proceedings of the National Academy of Sciences of the United States of America*, *113*(1), 200–205. https://www.pnas.org/doi/10.1073/pnas.1513619112
6. Kishida, K. T., Saez, I., Lohrenz, T., Witcher, M. R., Laxton, A. W., Tatter, S. B., White, J. P., Ellis, T. L., Phillips, P. E. M., & Montague, P. R. (2016). Subsecond dopamine fluctuations in human striatum encode superposed error signals about actual and counterfactual reward. *Proceedings of the National Academy of Sciences of the United States*

of America , *113*(1), 200–205. https://www.pnas.org/doi/10.1073/pnas.1513619112

7. Pignatiello, G. A., Martin, R. J., & Hickman, R. L. (2018). Decision fatigue: A conceptual analysis. *Journal of Health Psychology* , *25*(1), 123–135. https://www.ncbi.nlm.nih.gov/pmc/articles/PMC6119549/pdf/nihms956822.pdf

8. Tierney, J. (2011, August 17). Do you suffer from decision fatigue? *The New York Times Magazine*. Retrieved March 16, 2023, from https://www.nytimes.com/2011/08/21/magazine/do-you-suffer-from-decision-fatigue.html

9. Pignatiello, G. A., Martin, R. J., & Hickman, R. L. (2018). Decision fatigue: A conceptual analysis. *Journal of Health Psychology* , *25*(1), 123–135. https://www.ncbi.nlm.nih.gov/pmc/articles/PMC6119549/pdf/nihms956822.pdf

10. Tierney, J. (2011, August 17). Do you suffer from decision fatigue? *The New York Times Magazine*. Retrieved March 16, 2023, from https://www.nytimes.com/2011/08/21/magazine/do-you-suffer-from-decision-fatigue.html

11. Tierney, J. (2011, August 17). Do you suffer from decision fatigue? *The New York Times Magazine*. Retrieved March 16, 2023, from https://www.nytimes.com/2011/08/21/magazine/do-you-suffer-from-decision-fatigue.html

12. McKeown, J. (2014). *Essentialism: The disciplined pursuit of less*. Virgin Books.

13. Pignatiello, G. A., Martin, R. J., & Hickman, R. L. (2018). Decision fatigue: A conceptual analysis. *Journal of Health Psychology* , *25*(1), 123–135. https://www.ncbi.nlm.nih.gov/pmc/articles/PMC6119549/pdf/nihms956822.pdf

14. Pignatiello, G. A., Martin, R. J., & Hickman, R. L. (2018). Decision fatigue: A conceptual analysis. *Journal of Health Psychology* , *25*(1), 123–135. https://www.ncbi.nlm.nih.gov/pmc/articles/PMC6119549/pdf/nihms956822.pdf

15. Persson, E., Barrafrem, K., Meunier, A., & Tinghög, G. (2019). The effect of decision fatigue on surgeons' clinical decision making. *Health Economics, 28*, 1194–1203. https://doi.org/10.1002/hec.3933

16. Danziger, S., Levav, J., & Avnaim-Pesso, L. (2011). Extraneous factors in judicial decisions. *Proceedings of the National Academy of Sciences of the United States of America, 108*(17), 6889–6892. https://www.pnas.org/doi/10.1073/pnas.1018033108

2. The Battle For Attention

1. Pignatiello, G. A., Martin, R. J., & Hickman, R. L. (2018). Decision fatigue: A conceptual analysis. *Journal of Health Psychology* , *25*(1), 123–135. https://doi.org/https://www.ncbi.nlm.nih.gov/pmc/articles/PMC6119549/pdf/nihms956822.pdf

2. Cao, X., Guo, X., Vogel, D., & Zhang, X. (2016). Exploring the influence of social media on employee work performance. *Internet Research* , *26*(2). Retrieved from https://www.emerald.com/insight/content/doi/10.1108/IntR-11-2014-0299/full/html.

3. Cao, X., Guo, X., Vogel, D., & Zhang, X. (2016). Exploring the influence of social media on employee work performance. *Internet Research* , *26*(2). Retrieved from https://www.emerald.com/insight/content/doi/10.1108/IntR-11-2014-0299/full/html.

4. Clear, J. (n.d.). 40 years of stanford research found that people with this one quality are more likely to succeed. *James Clear*. Retrieved March 2023, from https://jamesclear.com/delayed-gratification

5. Konnikova, M. (2014, October 9). The struggles of a psychologist studying self-control . *The New Yorker*. Retrieved March 2023, from https://www.newyorker.com/science/maria-konnikova/struggles-psychologist-studying-self-control.

6. Clear, J. (n.d.). 40 years of stanford research found that people with this one quality are more likely to succeed. *James Clear*. Retrieved March 2023, from https://jamesclear.com/delayed-gratification

7. Konnikova, M. (2014, October 9). The struggles of a psychologist studying self-control . *The New Yorker*. Retrieved March 2023, from https://www.newyorker.com/science/maria-konnikova/struggles-psychologist-studying-self-control.

8. Carli, J. (2018, September 21). Remembrance for Walter Mischel, psychologist who devised the marshmallow test. *National Public Radio*. Retrieved March 2023, from https://www.npr.org/sections/health-shots/2018/09/21/650015068/remembrance-for-walter-mischel-psychologist-who-devised-the-marshmallow-test

9. Newport Institute. (2021, February 24). How does your physical environment affect you and your mental health? *Newport Institute*. Retrieved March 25, 2023, from https://www.newportinstitute.com/resources/mental-health/physical-environment-affect-you/

10. Newport Institute. (2021, February 24). How does your physical environment affect you and your mental health? *Newport Institute*. Retrieved March 25, 2023, from https://www.newportinstitute.com/resources/mental-health/physical-environment-affect-you/

11. Steinert, C., Heim, N., & Leichsenring, F. (2021). Procrastination, perfectionism, and other work-related mental problems: Prevalence, types, assessment, and treatment—a scoping review. *Frontiers in Psychiatry*, *12*. https://www.frontiersin.org/articles/10.3389/fpsyt.2021.736776/full

12. Cherry, K. (2022, November 14). What is procrastination? *Verywell Mind*. Retrieved March 28, 2023, from https://www.verywellmind.com/the-psychology-of-procrastination-2795944

13. Steinert, C., Heim, N., & Leichsenring, F. (2021). Procrastination, perfectionism, and other work-related mental problems: Prevalence, types, assessment, and treatment—a scoping review. *Frontiers in Psychiatry*, *12*. https://www.frontiersin.org/articles/10.3389/fpsyt.2021.736776/full

14. Cherry, K. (2022, November 14). What is procrastination? *Verywell Mind*. Retrieved March 28, 2023, from https://www.verywellmind.com/the-psychology-of-procrastination-2795944

15. Steinert, C., Heim, N., & Leichsenring, F. (2021). Procrastination, perfectionism, and other work-related mental problems: Prevalence, types, assessment, and treatment—a scoping review. *Frontiers in Psychiatry*, *12*. https://www.frontiersin.org/articles/10.3389/fpsyt.2021.736776/full

16. Romash, I. (2020). The nature of the manifestation of procrastination, level of anxiety and depression in medical students in a period of altered psycho-emotional state during forced social distancing because of pandemic COVID-19 and its impact on academic performance. *Mental Health: Global Challenges Journal* , *3*(2), 6 11. Retrieved March 28, 2023, from https://mhgcj.org/index.php/MHGCJ/article/view/92/81.

17. Steinert, C., Heim, N., & Leichsenring, F. (2021). Procrastination, perfectionism, and other work-related mental problems: Prevalence, types, assessment, and treatment—a scoping review. *Frontiers in Psychiatry*, *12*. https://www.frontiersin.org/articles/10.3389/fpsyt.2021.736776/full

18. Schulz van Endert, T., & Mohr, P. N. (2022). Delay discounting of monetary and social media rewards: Magnitude and trait effects. *Frontiers in Psychology*, *13*. https://www.frontiersin.org/articles/10.3389/fpsyg.2022.822505/full

19. Zahariades, D. (2017). *The procrastination cure: 21 proven tactics for conquering your inner procrastinator, mastering your time, and boosting your productivity!* Art of Productivity.

20. Cherry, K. (2022, November 14). What is procrastination? *Verywell Mind*. Retrieved March 28, 2023, from https://www.verywellmind.com/the-psychology-of-procrastination-2795944

21. Zahariades, D. (2017). *The procrastination cure: 21 proven tactics for conquering your inner procrastinator, mastering your time, and boosting your productivity!* Art of Productivity.

22. Cherry, K. (2022, November 14). What is procrastination? *Verywell Mind*. Retrieved March 28, 2023, from https://www.verywellmind.com/the-psychology-of-procrastination-2795944

23. Zahariades, D. (2017). *The procrastination cure: 21 proven tactics for conquering your inner procrastinator, mastering your time, and boosting your productivity!* Art of Productivity.

24. Cherry, K. (2022, November 14). What is procrastination? *Verywell Mind*. Retrieved March 28, 2023, from https://www.verywellmind.com/the-psychology-of-procrastination-2795944

25. Heitz, D. (2017, December 24). Perfectionism. *Healthline*. Retrieved March 28, 2023, from https://www.healthline.com/health/perfectionism#prevention

26. Steinert, C., Heim, N., & Leichsenring, F. (2021). Procrastination, perfectionism, and other work-related mental problems: Prevalence, types, assessment, and treatment—a scoping review. *Frontiers in Psychiatry*, *12*. https://www.frontiersin.org/articles/10.3389/fpsyt.2021.736776/full

27. Steinert, C., Heim, N., & Leichsenring, F. (2021). Procrastination, perfectionism, and other work-related mental problems: Prevalence, types, assessment, and treatment—a scoping review. *Frontiers in Psychiatry*, *12*. https://www.frontiersin.org/articles/10.3389/fpsyt.2021.736776/full

28. Heitz, D. (2017, December 24). Perfectionism. *Healthline*. Retrieved March 28, 2023, from https://www.healthline.com/health/perfectionism#prevention

29. Heitz, D. (2017, December 24). Perfectionism. *Healthline*. Retrieved March 28, 2023, from https://www.healthline.com/health/perfectionism#prevention

30. Cherry, K. (2022, November 14). What is procrastination? *Verywell Mind*. Retrieved March 28, 2023, from https://www.verywellmind.com/the-psychology-of-procrastination-2795944

31. Macit, H. B., Macit, G., & Güngör, O. (2018). A research on social media addiction and dopamine driven feedback. *Journal of Mehmet Akif Ersoy University Economics and Administrative Sciences Faculty*, 882-897. https://dergipark.org.tr/tr/download/article-file/607734

32. Kishida, K. T., Saez, I., Lohrenz, T., Witcher, M. R., Laxton, A. W., Tatter, S. B., White, J. P., Ellis, T. L., Phillips, P. E. M., & Montague, P. R. (2016). Subsecond dopamine fluctuations in human striatum encode superposed error signals about actual and counterfactual reward. *Proceedings of the National Academy of Sciences of the United States*

of America , *113*(1), 200 205. https://www.pnas.org/doi/10.1073/pnas.1513619112

33. Chen, X., Voets, S., Jenkinson, N., & Galea, J. M. (2020). Dopamine-Dependent loss aversion during effort-based decision making. *The Journal of Neuroscience*, *40*(3), 661 670. https://www.jneurosci.org/content/40/3/661

34. Caloia, D. (2022, September 2). Social media is shortening our attention spans. *The Journal*. Retrieved March 2023, from https://www.queensjournal.ca/story/2022-09-01/opinions/social-media-is-shortening-our-attention-spans/.

35. Zahariades, D. (2017). *The procrastination cure: 21 proven tactics for conquering your inner procrastinator, mastering your time, and boosting your productivity!* Art of Productivity.

36. Macit, H. B., Macit, G., & Güngör, O. (2018). A research on social media addiction and dopamine driven feedback. *Journal of Mehmet Akif Ersoy University Economics and Administrative Sciences Faculty*, 882 897. https://dergipark.org.tr/tr/download/article-file/607734

37. Chen, X., Voets, S., Jenkinson, N., & Galea, J. M. (2020). Dopamine-Dependent loss aversion during effort-based decision making. *The Journal of Neuroscience*, *40*(3), 661 670. https://www.jneurosci.org/content/40/3/661

38. Macit, H. B., Macit, G., & Güngör, O. (2018). A research on social media addiction and dopamine driven feedback. *Journal of Mehmet Akif Ersoy University Economics and Administrative Sciences Faculty*, 882 897. https://dergipark.org.tr/tr/download/article-file/607734

39. Caloia, D. (2022, September 2). Social media is shortening our attention spans. *The Journal*. Retrieved March 2023, from https://www.queensjournal.ca/story/2022-09-01/opinions/social-media-is-shortening-our-attention-spans/.

40. Macit, H. B., Macit, G., & Güngör, O. (2018). A research on social media addiction and dopamine driven feedback. *Journal of Mehmet Akif Ersoy University Economics and Administrative Sciences Faculty*, 882 897. https://doi.org/10.30798/makuiibf.435845

41. The Guardian. (2021, April 23). Is technology short-changing our attention spans? *The Guardian Labs*. Retrieved March 2023, from https://www.theguardian.com/sbs-on-demand--are-you-addicted-to-technology/2021/apr/23/is-technology-short-changing-our-attention-spans

3. The Myth Of Multitasking

1. Collins. Hustle. In *Collins English Dictionary*. Retrieved May 5, 2023, from https://www.collinsdictionary.com/us/dictionary/english/hustle#:

2. Merriam-Webster. (n.d.). Hustle. In *Merriam-Webster.com dictionary*. Retrieved April 1, 2023, from https://www.merriam-webster.com/dictionary/hustle

3. Oxford University Press. (n.d.). Hustle. In *Oxford Learner's Dictionaries*. Retrieved June 5, 2023, from https://www.oxfordlearners dictionaries.com/definition/american_english/hustle_1#:~:text=%5Btransitive%2C%20intransitive%5D%20hus-tle%20(,with%20a%20lot%20of%20energy

4. McKeown, J. (2014). *Essentialism: The disciplined pursuit of less*. Virgin Books.

5. Newport, C. (2016). *Deep work: Rules for focused success in a distracted world: Rules for focused success in a distracted world* (1st ed., Ser. ebook). Grand Central Publishing.

6. Newport, C. (2016). *Deep work: Rules for focused success in a distracted world: Rules for focused success in a distracted world* (1st ed., Ser. ebook). Grand Central Publishing.

7. Merriam-Webster. (n.d.). Productive. In *Merriam-Webster.com dictionary*. Retrieved April 2, 2023, from https://www.merriam-webster.com/dictionary/productive

8. The Guardian. (2021, April 23). Is technology short-changing our attention spans? *The Guardian Labs.* Retrieved March 2023, from https://www.theguardian.com/sbs-on-demand--are-you-addicted-to-technology/2021/apr/23/is-technology-short-changing-our-attention-spans

9. Leitão, J., Pereira, D., & Gonçalves, Â. (2019). Quality of Work Life and organizational performance: Workers' feelings of contributing, or not, to the organization's productivity. *International Journal of Environmental Research and Public Health, 16*(20), 3803. https://doi.org/10.3390/ijerph16203803

10. Newport, C. (2016). *Deep work: Rules for focused success in a distracted world: Rules for focused success in a distracted world* (1st ed., Ser. ebook). Grand Central Publishing.

11. Leitão, J., Pereira, D., & Gonçalves, Â. (2019). Quality of Work Life and organizational performance: Workers' feelings of contributing, or not, to the organization's productivity. *International Journal of Environmental Research and Public Health, 16*(20), 3803. https://doi.org/10.3390/ijerph16203803

12. Raub, S., & Blunschi, S. (2014). The power of meaningful work: How awareness of CSR initiatives fosters task significance and positive work outcomes in service employees. *Cornell Hospitality Quarterly*, *55*(1), 10–18. https://doi.org/10.1177/1938965513498300

13. Leitão, J., Pereira, D., & Gonçalves, Â. (2019). Quality of Work Life and organizational performance: Workers' feelings of contributing, or not, to the organization's productivity. *International Journal of Environmental Research and Public Health*, *16*(20), 3803. https://doi.org/10.3390/ijerph16203803

14. Pereira, D., Leitão, J., & Ramos, L. (2022). Burnout and quality of work life among municipal workers: Do motivating and economic factors play a mediating role? *International Journal of Environmental Research and Public Health*, *19*(20), 13035. https://doi.org/10.3390/ijerph192013035

15. Leitão, J., Pereira, D., & Gonçalves, Â. (2019). Quality of Work Life and organizational performance: Workers' feelings of contributing, or not, to the organization's productivity. *International Journal of Environmental Research and Public Health*, *16*(20), 3803. https://doi.org/10.3390/ijerph16203803

16. Pereira, D., Leitão, J., & Ramos, L. (2022). Burnout and quality of work life among municipal workers: Do motivating and economic factors play a mediating role? *International Journal of Environmental Research and Public Health*, *19*(20), 13035. https://doi.org/10.3390/ijerph192013035

17. Vahedasrami, M. J., Tabari, M., & Mehrara, A. (2022). Model of reducing job burnout in human resources in state organizations using a meta-synthesis approach. *Public Management Researches*, *15*(56), 225–254. https://doi.org/10.22111/JMR.2021.40168.5622

18. World Health Organization. (2023). *Burn-out an "Occupational phenomenon": International Classification of Diseases.* World Health Organization. Retrieved April 2, 2023, from https://www.who.int/news/item/28-05-2019-burn-out-an-occupational-phenomenon-international-classification-of-diseases

19. Pereira, D., Leitão, J., & Ramos, L. (2022). Burnout and quality of work life among municipal workers: Do motivating and economic factors play a mediating role? *International Journal of Environmental Research and Public Health*, *19*(20), 13035. https://doi.org/10.3390/ijerph192013035

20. Hamidi, Y., Fayazi, N., Soltanian, A., Heidari, G., Ahmadpanah, M., & Nazari, N. et al. (2107). Relationship between occupational stress and the performance of health care units in Hamadan Health

Center, Iran. *johe 4*(3), 26-32. http://johe.umsha.ac.ir/article-1-317-en.html

21. Vahedasrami, M. J., Tabari, M., & Mehrara, A. (2022). Model of reducing job burnout in human resources in state organizations using a meta-synthesis approach. *Public Management Researches*, *15*(56), 225–254. https://doi.org/10.22111/JMR.2021.40168.5622

22. Pereira, D., Leitão, J., & Ramos, L. (2022). Burnout and quality of work life among municipal workers: Do motivating and economic factors play a mediating role? *International Journal of Environmental Research and Public Health*, *19*(20), 13035. https://doi.org/10.3390/ijerph192013035

23. Thomas, M. (2022, July 27). What does work-life balance even mean? *Forbes*. Retrieved May 6, 2023, from https://www.forbes.com/sites/maurathomas/2022/07/26/what-does-work-life-balance-even-mean/?sh=3d9a35172617

24. Gharagozlou F., Karamimatin, B, Kashefi, H., Nikravesh Babaei, D., Bakhtyarizadeh, F., Rahimi, S. (2020). *The relationship between quality of working life of nurses in educational hospitals of Kermanshah with their perception and evaluation of workload in 2017.* Iran Occupational Health, *17*(3), 25-36. Retrieved April 1, 2023 from https://ioh.iums.ac.ir/article-1-2333-en.pdf

25. Pereira, D., Leitão, J., & Ramos, L. (2022). Burnout and quality of work life among municipal workers: Do motivating and economic factors play a mediating role? *International Journal of Environmental Research and Public Health*, *19*(20), 13035. https://doi.org/10.3390/ijerph192013035

26. Thomas, M. (2022, July 27). What does work-life balance even mean? *Forbes*. Retrieved May 6, 2023, from https://www.forbes.com/sites/maurathomas/2022/07/26/what-does-work-life-balance-even-mean/?sh=3d9a35172617

27. Vahedasrami, M. J., Tabari, M., & Mehrara, A. (2022). Model of reducing job burnout in human resources in state organizations using a meta-synthesis approach. *Public Management Researches*, *15*(56), 225–254. https://doi.org/10.22111/JMR.2021.40168.5622

28. Pereira, D., Leitão, J., & Ramos, L. (2022). Burnout and quality of work life among municipal workers: Do motivating and economic factors play a mediating role? *International Journal of Environmental Research and Public Health*, *19*(20), 13035. https://doi.org/10.3390/ijerph192013035

29. Vahedasrami, M. J., Tabari, M., & Mehrara, A. (2022). Model of reducing job burnout in human resources in state organizations using a meta-synthesis approach. *Public Management Researches*, *15*(56), 225–254. https://doi.org/10.22111/JMR.2021.40168.5622

30. Pereira, D., Leitão, J., & Ramos, L. (2022). Burnout and quality of work life among municipal workers: Do motivating and economic factors play a mediating role? *International Journal of Environmental Research and Public Health, 19*(20), 13035. https://doi.org/10.3390/ijerph192013035

31. Vahedasrami, M. J., Tabari, M., & Mehrara, A. (2022). Model of reducing job burnout in human resources in state organizations using a meta-synthesis approach. *Public Management Researches, 15*(56), 225–254. https://doi.org/10.22111/JMR.2021.40168.5622

32. Newport, C. (2016). *Deep work: Rules for focused success in a distracted world: Rules for focused success in a distracted world* (1st ed., Ser. ebook). Grand Central Publishing.

33. Vahedasrami, M. J., Tabari, M., & Mehrara, A. (2022). Model of reducing job burnout in human resources in state organizations using a meta-synthesis approach. *Public Management Researches, 15*(56), 225–254. https://doi.org/10.22111/JMR.2021.40168.5622

34. Newport, C. (2016). *Deep work: Rules for focused success in a distracted world: Rules for focused success in a distracted world* (1st ed., Ser. ebook). Grand Central Publishing.

35. Morgan, E. (2021, October 22). How to retrain your frazzled brain and find your focus again. *The Guardian.* Retrieved May 5, 2023, from https://www.theguardian.com/lifeandstyle/2021/oct/22/how-to-retrain-your-frazzled-brain-and-find-your-focus-again

36. Thomas, M. (2022, July 27). What does work-life balance even mean? *Forbes.* Retrieved May 6, 2023, from https://www.forbes.com/sites/maurathomas/2022/07/26/what-does-work-life-balance-even-mean/?sh=3d9a35172617

37. Morgan, E. (2021, October 22). How to retrain your frazzled brain and find your focus again. *The Guardian.* Retrieved May 5, 2023, from https://www.theguardian.com/lifeandstyle/2021/oct/22/how-to-retrain-your-frazzled-brain-and-find-your-focus-again

38. Diaz, B. A., Van Der Sluis, S., Moens, S., Benjamins, J. S., Migliorati, F., Stoffers, D., Den Braber, A., Poil, S.-S., Hardstone, R., Van't Ent, D., Boomsma, D. I., De Geus, E., Mansvelder, H. D., Van Someren, E. J., & Linkenkaer-Hansen, K. (2013). The Amsterdam resting-state questionnaire reveals multiple phenotypes of resting-state cognition. *Frontiers in Human Neuroscience, 7.* https://doi.org/10.3389/fnhum.2013.00446

39. Morgan, E. (2021, October 22). How to retrain your frazzled brain and find your focus again. *The Guardian.* Retrieved May 5, 2023, from https://www.theguardian.com/lifeandstyle/2021/oct/22/how-to-retrain-your-frazzled-brain-and-find-your-focus-again

40. Tsuei, J. (2023). Deep work' tips to improve your focus & productivity: Clockwise. *Clockwise.* https://www.getclockwise.com/blog/tips-for-how-to-deep-work

41. Newport, C. (2016). *Deep work: Rules for focused success in a distracted world* (1st ed., Ser. ebook). Grand Central Publishing.

42. Tsuei, J. (2023). Deep work' tips to improve your focus & productivity: Clockwise. *Clockwise.* https://www.getclockwise.com/blog/tips-for-how-to-deep-work

43. Newport, C. (2016). *Deep work: Rules for focused success in a distracted world* (1st ed., Ser. ebook). Grand Central Publishing.

44. Tsuei, J. (2023). Deep work' tips to improve your focus & productivity: Clockwise. *Clockwise.* https://www.getclockwise.com/blog/tips-for-how-to-deep-work

45. Newport, C. (2016). *Deep work: Rules for focused success in a distracted world* (1st ed., Ser. ebook). Grand Central Publishing.

46. Tsuei, J. (2023). Deep work' tips to improve your focus & productivity: Clockwise. *Clockwise.* https://www.getclockwise.com/blog/tips-for-how-to-deep-work

47. McKeown, J. (2014). *Essentialism: The disciplined pursuit of less.* Virgin Books.

48. McKeown, J. (2014). *Essentialism: The disciplined pursuit of less.* Virgin Books.

49. Wilding, M. (2021, September 20). *How to say "no" after saying "yes".* Harvard Business Review. Retrieved May 5, 2023, from https://hbr.org/2021/09/how-to-say-no-after-saying-yes

50. Merriam-Webster. (n.d.). Productive. In *Merriam-Webster.com dictionary.* Retrieved April 2, 2023, from https://www.merriam-webster.com/dictionary/productive

4. The Power Of The Pause

1. Tippet, K. (2021, January 21). Katherine May How 'wintering' replenishes. *The On Being Project.* Retrieved April 25, 2023, from https://onbeing.org/programs/katherine-may-how-wintering-replenishes/.

2. Tippet, K. (2021, January 21). Katherine May How 'wintering' replenishes. *The On Being Project.* Retrieved April 25, 2023, from https://onbeing.org/programs/katherine-may-how-wintering-replenishes/.

3. Eastwood, J. D., Frischen, A., Fenske, M. J., & Smilek, D. (2012). The unengaged mind: Defining boredom in terms of attention.

Perspectives on Psychological Science, 7(5), 482–495. http://www.jstor.org/stable/44280796

4. Eastwood, J. D., Frischen, A., Fenske, M. J., & Smilek, D. (2012). The unengaged mind: Defining boredom in terms of attention. *Perspectives on Psychological Science, 7*(5), 482–495. http://www.jstor.org/stable/44280796

5. Rodriguez McRobbie, L. (2012, November 20). The history of boredom. *Smithsonian.com.* Retrieved April 24, 2023, from https://www.smithsonianmag.com/science-nature/the-history-of-boredom-138176427/

6. Microsoft. (2021, April 20). *Research proves your brain needs breaks.* Microsoft. Retrieved April 6, 2023, from https://www.microsoft.com/en-us/worklab/work-trend-index/brain-research

7. Thomas, J., Jamieson, G., & Cohen, M. (2014). Low and then high frequency oscillations of distinct right cortical networks are progressively enhanced by medium and long term Satyananda Yoga Meditation Practice. *Frontiers in Human Neuroscience, 8.* https://doi.org/10.3389/fnhum.2014.00197

8. Diaz, B. A., Van Der Sluis, S., Moens, S., Benjamins, J. S., Migliorati, F., Stoffers, D., Den Braber, A., Poil, S.-S., Hardstone, R., Van't Ent, D., Boomsma, D. I., De Geus, E., Mansvelder, H. D., Van Someren, E. J., & Linkenkaer-Hansen, K. (2013). The Amsterdam resting-state questionnaire reveals multiple phenotypes of resting-state cognition. *Frontiers in Human Neuroscience, 7.* https://doi.org/10.3389/fnhum.2013.00446

9. Eastwood, J. D., Frischen, A., Fenske, M. J., & Smilek, D. (2012). The unengaged mind: Defining boredom in terms of attention. *Perspectives on Psychological Science, 7*(5), 482–495. http://www.jstor.org/stable/44280796

10. Diaz, B. A., Van Der Sluis, S., Moens, S., Benjamins, J. S., Migliorati, F., Stoffers, D., Den Braber, A., Poil, S.-S., Hardstone, R., Van't Ent, D., Boomsma, D. I., De Geus, E., Mansvelder, H. D., Van Someren, E. J., & Linkenkaer-Hansen, K. (2013). The Amsterdam resting-state questionnaire reveals multiple phenotypes of resting-state cognition. *Frontiers in Human Neuroscience, 7.* https://doi.org/10.3389/fnhum.2013.00446

11. Eastwood, J. D., Frischen, A., Fenske, M. J., & Smilek, D. (2012). The unengaged mind: Defining boredom in terms of attention. *Perspectives on Psychological Science, 7*(5), 482–495. http://www.jstor.org/stable/44280796

12. Diaz, B. A., Van Der Sluis, S., Moens, S., Benjamins, J. S., Migliorati, F., Stoffers, D., Den Braber, A., Poil, S.-S., Hardstone, R., Van't Ent, D., Boomsma, D. I., De Geus, E., Mansvelder, H. D.,

Van Someren, E. J., & Linkenkaer-Hansen, K. (2013). The Amsterdam resting-state questionnaire reveals multiple phenotypes of resting-state cognition. *Frontiers in Human Neuroscience*, *7*. https://doi.org/10.3389/fnhum.2013.00446

13. Thomas, J., Jamieson, G., & Cohen, M. (2014). Low and then high frequency oscillations of distinct right cortical networks are progressively enhanced by medium and long term Satyananda Yoga Meditation Practice. *Frontiers in Human Neuroscience*, *8*. https://doi.org/10.3389/fnhum.2014.00197

14. Trenton, N. (2021). *Stop overthinking: 23 techniques to relieve stress, stop negative spirals, declutter your mind, and focus on the present*. Pkcs Media, Inc.

15. Gan, Q., Ding, N., Bi, G., Liu, R., Zhao, X., Zhong, J., Wu, S., Zeng, Y., Cui, L., Wu, K., Fu, Y., & Chen, Z. (2022). Enhanced resting-state functional connectivity with decreased amplitude of low-frequency fluctuations of the salience network in mindfulness novices. *Frontiers in Human Neuroscience*, *16*. https://doi.org/10.3389/fnhum.2022.838123

16. Thomas, J., Jamieson, G., & Cohen, M. (2014). Low and then high frequency oscillations of distinct right cortical networks are progressively enhanced by medium and long term Satyananda Yoga Meditation Practice. *Frontiers in Human Neuroscience*, *8*. https://doi.org/10.3389/fnhum.2014.00197

17. Gizewski, E. R., Steiger, R., Waibel, M., Pereverzyev, S., Sommer, P. J., Siedentopf, C., Grams, A. E., Lenhart, L., & Singewald, N. (2020). Short-term meditation training influences Brain Energy Metabolism: A pilot study on 31 P mr spectroscopy. *Brain and Behavior*, *11*(1). https://doi.org/10.1002/brb3.1914

18. Newport, C. (2016). *Deep work: Rules for focused success in a distracted world* (1st ed., Ser. ebook). Grand Central Publishing.

19. Gan, Q., Ding, N., Bi, G., Liu, R., Zhao, X., Zhong, J., Wu, S., Zeng, Y., Cui, L., Wu, K., Fu, Y., & Chen, Z. (2022). Enhanced resting-state functional connectivity with decreased amplitude of low-frequency fluctuations of the salience network in mindfulness novices. *Frontiers in Human Neuroscience*, *16*. https://doi.org/10.3389/fnhum.2022.838123

20. Thomas, J., Jamieson, G., & Cohen, M. (2014). Low and then high frequency oscillations of distinct right cortical networks are progressively enhanced by medium and long term Satyananda Yoga Meditation Practice. *Frontiers in Human Neuroscience*, *8*. https://doi.org/10.3389/fnhum.2014.00197

21. Gan, Q., Ding, N., Bi, G., Liu, R., Zhao, X., Zhong, J., Wu, S., Zeng, Y., Cui, L., Wu, K., Fu, Y., & Chen, Z. (2022). Enhanced

resting-state functional connectivity with decreased amplitude of low-frequency fluctuations of the salience network in mindfulness novices. *Frontiers in Human Neuroscience*, 16. https://doi.org/10.3389/fnhum.2022.838123

22. Mascaro, J. S., Darcher, A., Negi, L. T., & Raison, C. L. (2015). The neural mediators of kindness-based meditation: A theoretical model. *Frontiers in Psychology*, 6. https://doi.org/10.3389/fpsyg.2015.00109

23. Gan, Q., Ding, N., Bi, G., Liu, R., Zhao, X., Zhong, J., Wu, S., Zeng, Y., Cui, L., Wu, K., Fu, Y., & Chen, Z. (2022). Enhanced resting-state functional connectivity with decreased amplitude of low-frequency fluctuations of the salience network in mindfulness novices. *Frontiers in Human Neuroscience*, 16. https://doi.org/10.3389/fnhum.2022.838123

24. Bird, M. (2022, February 8). *Maximizing your creativity with productive meditation*. Objective Standard Institute. Retrieved April 14, 2023, from https://objectivestandard.org/blog/maximizing-your-creativity-with-productive-meditation

25. Bird, M. (2022, February 8). *Maximizing your creativity with productive meditation*. Objective Standard Institute. Retrieved April 14, 2023, from https://objectivestandard.org/blog/maximizing-your-creativity-with-productive-meditation

26. Butler, A. (n.d.). Why productive meditation should be on your to-do list. *Primal Storytelling*. Retrieved April 14, 2023, from https://info.primalstorytelling.com/blog/why-productive-meditation-should-be-on-your-to-do-list

27. Bird, M. (2022, February 8). *Maximizing your creativity with productive meditation*. Objective Standard Institute. Retrieved April 14, 2023, from https://objectivestandard.org/blog/maximizing-your-creativity-with-productive-meditation

28. Butler, A. (n.d.). Why productive meditation should be on your to-do list. *Primal Storytelling*. Retrieved April 14, 2023, from https://info.primalstorytelling.com/blog/why-productive-meditation-should-be-on-your-to-do-list

29. Bird, M. (2022, February 8). *Maximizing your creativity with productive meditation*. Objective Standard Institute. Retrieved April 14, 2023, from https://objectivestandard.org/blog/maximizing-your-creativity-with-productive-meditation

30. Butler, A. (n.d.). Why productive meditation should be on your to-do list. *Primal Storytelling*. Retrieved April 14, 2023, from https://info.primalstorytelling.com/blog/why-productive-meditation-should-be-on-your-to-do-list

31. Bird, M. (2022, February 8). *Maximizing your creativity with productive meditation.* Objective Standard Institute. Retrieved April 14, 2023, from https://objectivestandard.org/blog/maximizing-your-creativity-with-productive-meditation

32. Butler, A. (n.d.). Why productive meditation should be on your to-do list. *Primal Storytelling.* Retrieved April 14, 2023, from https://info.primalstorytelling.com/blog/why-productive-meditation-should-be-on-your-to-do-list

33. Bird, M. (2022, February 8). *Maximizing your creativity with productive meditation.* Objective Standard Institute. Retrieved April 14, 2023, from https://objectivestandard.org/blog/maximizing-your-creativity-with-productive-meditation

34. Annear, S. (2020, August 10). Routines and 'shutdown rituals' help maintain a balance between work and life during COVID-19 - The Boston Globe. *BostonGlobe.com.* Retrieved April 4, 2023, from https://www.bostonglobe.com/2020/08/06/nation/trying-separate-life-work-while-stuck-home-during-covid-19-develop-shutdown-ritual/

35. Jack Frederick @workingatduke, & Frederick, J. (2022, January 26). *How end of workday routines make a difference.* Duke Today. Retrieved April 4, 2023, from https://today.duke.edu/2022/01/how-end-workday-routines-make-difference

36. Newport, C. (2023, January 26). Drastically reduce stress with a work shutdown ritual. *Cal Newport.* Retrieved April 4, 2023, from https://calnewport.com/drastically-reduce-stress-with-a-work-shutdown-ritual/

37. Newport, C. (2023, January 26). Drastically reduce stress with a work shutdown ritual. *Cal Newport.* Retrieved April 4, 2023, from https://calnewport.com/drastically-reduce-stress-with-a-work-shutdown-ritual/

38. Newport, C. (2023, January 26). Drastically reduce stress with a work shutdown ritual. *Cal Newport.* Retrieved April 4, 2023, from https://calnewport.com/drastically-reduce-stress-with-a-work-shutdown-ritual/

39. Jack Frederick @workingatduke, & Frederick, J. (2022, January 26). *How end of workday routines make a difference.* Duke Today. Retrieved April 4, 2023, from https://today.duke.edu/2022/01/how-end-workday-routines-make-difference

40. McKeown, G. (2021). *Effortless make it easier to do what matters most.* Virgin Books.

5. Make Better Decisions Through Focus

1. Trenton, N. (2021). *Stop overthinking: 23 techniques to relieve stress, stop negative spirals, declutter your mind, and focus on the present.* Pkcs Media, Inc.
2. Newport Institute. (2021, February 24). How does your physical environment affect you and your mental health? *Newport Institute.* Retrieved March 25, 2023, from https://www.newportinstitute. com/resources/mental-health/physical-environment-affect-you/
3. Pirmoradi, Z., Golmohammadi, R., Motamedzade, M., Faradmal, J. Assessing lighting and color temperature in the office workplaces and relationship to visual comfort. ioh, *17*(1), 1-10. http://ioh.iums. ac.ir/article-1-2387-en.html
4. Newport Institute. (2021, February 24). How does your physical environment affect you and your mental health? *Newport Institute.* Retrieved March 25, 2023, from https://www.newportinstitute. com/resources/mental-health/physical-environment-affect-you/
5. Pirmoradi, Z., Golmohammadi, R., Motamedzade, M., Faradmal, J. Assessing lighting and color temperature in the office workplaces and relationship to visual comfort. ioh, *17*(1), 1-10. http://ioh.iums. ac.ir/article-1-2387-en.html
6. Newport Institute. (2021, February 24). How does your physical environment affect you and your mental health? *Newport Institute.* Retrieved March 25, 2023, from https://www.newportinstitute. com/resources/mental-health/physical-environment-affect-you/
7. BrainFM, Inc. (2023). *Music to focus better.* https://www.brain.fm/
8. Newport Institute. (2021, February 24). How does your physical environment affect you and your mental health? *Newport Institute.* Retrieved March 25, 2023, from https://www.newportinstitute. com/resources/mental-health/physical-environment-affect-you/
9. Newport Institute. (2021, February 24). How does your physical environment affect you and your mental health? *Newport Institute.* Retrieved March 25, 2023, from https://www.newportinstitute. com/resources/mental-health/physical-environment-affect-you/
10. Cherry, K. (2022, November 14). What is procrastination? *Verywell Mind.* Retrieved March 28, 2023, from https://www.verywellmind. com/the-psychology-of-procrastination-2795944
11. Zahariades, D. (2017). *The procrastination cure: 21 proven tactics for conquering your inner procrastinator, mastering your time, and boosting your productivity!* Art of Productivity.
12. Cherry, K. (2022, November 14). What is procrastination? *Verywell Mind.* Retrieved March 28, 2023, from https://www.verywellmind.

com/the-psychology-of-procrastination-2795944

13. Newport, C. (2016). *Deep work: Rules for focused success in a distracted world: Rules for focused success in a distracted world* (1st ed., Ser. ebook). Grand Central Publishing.

14. Zahariades, D. (2017). *The procrastination cure: 21 proven tactics for conquering your inner procrastinator, mastering your time, and boosting your productivity!* Art of Productivity.

15. Kishida, K. T., Saez, I., Lohrenz, T., Witcher, M. R., Laxton, A. W., Tatter, S. B., White, J. P., Ellis, T. L., Phillips, P. E. M., & Montague, P. R. (2016). Subsecond dopamine fluctuations in human striatum encode superposed error signals about actual and counterfactual reward. *Proceedings of the National Academy of Sciences of the United States of America , 113*(1), 200 205. https://www.pnas.org/doi/10.1073/pnas.1513619112

16. Trenton, N. (2021). *Stop overthinking: 23 techniques to relieve stress, stop negative spirals, declutter your mind, and focus on the present.* Pkcs Media, Inc.

17. Steinert, C., Heim, N., & Leichsenring, F. (2021). Procrastination, perfectionism, and other work-related mental problems: Prevalence, types, assessment, and treatment—a scoping review. *Frontiers in Psychiatry, 12.* https://doi.org/10.3389/fpsyt.2021.736776

18. Trenton, N. (2021). *Stop overthinking: 23 techniques to relieve stress, stop negative spirals, declutter your mind, and focus on the present.* Pkcs Media, Inc.

19. Alan Conway, M. D. (2022, August 25). *The 4 A's of stress relief.* Mayo Clinic Health System. Retrieved April 19, 2023, from https://www.mayoclinichealthsystem.org/hometown-health/speaking-of-health/the-4-as-of-stress-relief

20. Trenton, N. (2021). *Stop overthinking: 23 techniques to relieve stress, stop negative spirals, declutter your mind, and focus on the present.* Pkcs Media, Inc.

21. Pavlik, T. (2022, November 28). *Unwind this Monday with the 5-4-3-2-1 grounding technique.* The Monday Campaigns. Retrieved April 19, 2023, from https://www.mondaycampaigns.org/destress-monday/unwind-monday-5-4-3-2-1-grounding-technique

22. Lawson, J., Gander, S., Star, S. R. N., Kipling, S., & Macpherson, K. (2022). Making sense of mindfulness. In Lawson, J. E. (Ed.), *Teacher, take care: A guide to well-being and workplace wellness for educators* (pp. 43 58). Portage & Main Press.

23. TEDx. (2019, May 31). *How I overcame decision paralysis* [Video]. YouTube. Retrieved April 20, 2023, from https://www.youtube.com/watch?v=K9yDyl_LX4E.

24. Kishida, K. T., Saez, I., Lohrenz, T., Witcher, M. R., Laxton, A. W., Tatter, S. B., White, J. P., Ellis, T. L., Phillips, P. E. M., & Montague, P. R. (2016). Subsecond dopamine fluctuations in human striatum encode superposed error signals about actual and counterfactual reward. *Proceedings of the National Academy of Sciences of the United States of America* , *113*(1), 200–205. https://www.pnas.org/doi/10.1073/pnas.1513619112

25. Chen, X., Voets, S., Jenkinson, N., & Galea, J. M. (2020). Dopamine-dependent loss aversion during effort-based decision making. *The Journal of Neuroscience*, *40*(3), 661–670. https://doi.org/10.1523/jneurosci.1760-19.2019

26. University of Maryland School of Business. (2015, May 5). *Fighting decision fatigue* [Video]. YouTube. Retrieved April 20, 2023, from https://www.youtube.com/watch?v=NFsVqFF0gTc

6. Making Decisions With Less Energy

1. McKeown, J. (2014). *Essentialism: The disciplined pursuit of less*. Virgin Books.

2. Vahedasrami, M. J., Tabari, M., & Mehrara, A. (2022). Model of reducing job burnout in human resources in state organizations using a meta-synthesis approach. *Public Management Researches*, *15*(56), 225–254. https://doi.org/10.22111/JMR.2021.40168.5622

3. McKeown, J. (2014). *Essentialism: The disciplined pursuit of less*. Virgin Books.

4. McKeown, J. (2014). *Essentialism: The disciplined pursuit of less*. Virgin Books.

5. University of Maryland School of Business. (2015, May 5). *Fighting decision fatigue* [Video]. YouTube. Retrieved April 20, 2023, from https://www.youtube.com/watch?v=NFsVqFF0gT

6. McKeown, G. (2021). *Effortless make it easier to do what matters most*. Virgin Books.

7. McKeown, J. (2014). *Essentialism: The disciplined pursuit of less*. Virgin Books.

8. University of Maryland School of Business. (2015, May 5). *Fighting decision fatigue* [Video]. YouTube. Retrieved April 20, 2023, from https://www.youtube.com/watch?v=NFsVqFF0gT

9. McKeown, G. (2021). *Effortless make it easier to do what matters most*. Virgin Books.

10. Newport, C. (2016). *Deep work: Rules for focused success in a distracted world: Rules for focused success in a distracted world* (1st ed., Scr. ebook).

Grand Central Publishing.

11. University of Maryland School of Business. (2015, May 5). *Fighting decision fatigue* [Video]. YouTube. Retrieved April 20, 2023, from https://www.youtube.com/watch?v=NFsVqFF0gT

12. Zahariades, D. (2017). *The procrastination cure: 21 proven tactics for conquering your inner procrastinator, mastering your time, and boosting your productivity!* Art of Productivity.

13. University of Maryland School of Business. (2015, May 5). *Fighting decision fatigue* [Video]. YouTube. Retrieved April 20, 2023, from https://www.youtube.com/watch?v=NFsVqFF0gT

14. TEDx. (2019, May 31). *How I overcame decision paralysis* [Video]. YouTube. Retrieved April 20, 2023, from https://www.youtube.com/watch?v=K9yDyl_LX4E.

7. Making Purposeful Decisions

1. Chakraborty, S. (2020, May 30). *7 Confucius Quotes on Education that Changed the World*. Happenings@LPU. Retrieved April 23, 2023, from https://happenings.lpu.in/confucius-quotes-on-education-changed-world/

2. Pereira, D., Leitão, J., & Ramos, L. (2022). Burnout and quality of Work Life Among Municipal Workers: Do motivating and economic factors play a mediating role? *International Journal of Environmental Research and Public Health*, *19*(20), 13035. https://doi.org/10.3390/ijerph192013035

3. Newport, C. (2016). *Deep work: Rules for focused success in a distracted world: Rules for focused success in a distracted world* (1st ed., Ser. ebook). Grand Central Publishing.

4. Tsuei , J. (2023). Deep work' tips to improve your focus & productivity: Clockwise. *RSS*. Retrieved April 23, 2023, from https://www.getclockwise.com/blog/tips-for-how-to-deep-work

5. Newport, C. (2016). *Deep work: Rules for focused success in a distracted world: Rules for focused success in a distracted world* (1st ed., Ser. ebook). Grand Central Publishing.

6. McKeown, G. (2021). *Effortless make it easier to do what matters most.* Virgin Books.

7. Westaway, K. (2021, April 29). *Summary of effortless by Greg McKeown.* Forbes. https://www.forbes.com/sites/kylewestaway/2021/04/29/summary-of-effortless-by-greg-mckeown/?sh=27455dcc22e6

8. McKeown, G. (2021). *Effortless make it easier to do what matters most.* Virgin Books.

9. McKeown, G. (2021, June 19). *51. rest: The art of doing nothing - Greg McKeown*. Greg McKeown - Greg McKeown author and speaker. https://gregmckeown.com/podcast/episode/rest-the-art-of-doing-nothing/

10. Zhang, Q., Liao, Y., Qi, J., Zhao, Y., Zhu, T., Liu, Z., & Liu, X. (2014). A visual ERP study of impulse inhibition following a zaleplon-induced nap after sleep deprivation. *PLoS ONE*, *9*(5). https://doi.org/10.1371/journal.pone.0095653

11. Silva, J. (2021, July 8). *Effortless by Greg McKeown summary*. Jeremy Silva. https://jsilva.blog/2021/06/21/effortless-summary/

12. McKeown, G. (2021, June 19). *51. rest: The art of doing nothing - Greg McKeown*. Greg McKeown - Greg McKeown author and speaker. https://gregmckeown.com/podcast/episode/rest-the-art-of-doing-nothing/

13. Zhang, Q., Liao, Y., Qi, J., Zhao, Y., Zhu, T., Liu, Z., & Liu, X. (2014). A visual ERP study of impulse inhibition following a zaleplon-induced nap after sleep deprivation. *PLoS ONE*, *9*(5). https://doi.org/10.1371/journal.pone.0095653

14. Silva, J. (2021, July 8). *Effortless by Greg McKeown summary*. Jeremy Silva. https://jsilva.blog/2021/06/21/effortless-summary/

15. Morgan, E. (2021, October 22). How to retrain your frazzled brain and find your focus again. *The Guardian*. Retrieved May 5, 2023, from https://www.theguardian.com/lifeandstyle/2021/oct/22/how-to-retrain-your-frazzled-brain-and-find-your-focus-again

16. Westaway, K. (2021, April 29). *Summary of effortless by Greg McKeown*. Forbes. https://www.forbes.com/sites/kylewestaway/2021/04/29/summary-of-effortless-by-greg-mckeown/?sh=27455dcc22e6

17. McKeown, G. (2021). *Effortless make it easier to do what matters most*. Virgin Books.

18. McKeown, G. (2021). *Effortless make it easier to do what matters most*. Virgin Books.

19. Westaway, K. (2021, April 29). *Summary of effortless by Greg McKeown*. Forbes. https://www.forbes.com/sites/kylewestaway/2021/04/29/summary-of-effortless-by-greg-mckeown/?sh=27455dcc22e6

20. McKeown, G. (2021, June 19). *51. rest: The art of doing nothing - Greg McKeown*. Greg McKeown - Greg McKeown author and speaker. https://gregmckeown.com/podcast/episode/rest-the-art-of-doing-nothing/

21. Silva, J. (2021, July 8). *Effortless by Greg McKeown summary*. Jeremy Silva. https://jsilva.blog/2021/06/21/effortless-summary/

22. Newport, C. (2016). *Deep work: Rules for focused success in a distracted world: Rules for focused success in a distracted world* (1st ed., Ser. ebook). Grand Central Publishing.

23. Silva, J. (2021, July 8). *Effortless by Greg McKeown summary*. Jeremy Silva. https://jsilva.blog/2021/06/21/effortless-summary/

24. Westaway, K. (2021, April 29). *Summary of effortless by Greg McKeown*. Forbes. https://www.forbes.com/sites/kylewestaway/2021/04/29/summary-of-effortless-by-greg-mckeown/?sh=27455dcc22e6

25. Silva, J. (2021, July 8). *Effortless by Greg McKeown summary*. Jeremy Silva. https://jsilva.blog/2021/06/21/effortless-summary/

26. Dweck, C. (2023, April 6). What having a "growth mindset" actually means. *Harvard Business Review*. https://hbr.org/2016/01/what-having-a-growth-mindset-actually-means?registration=success

27. Dweck, C. (2023, April 6). What having a "growth mindset" actually means. *Harvard Business Review*. https://hbr.org/2016/01/what-having-a-growth-mindset-actually-means?registration=success

28. Dweck, C. (2023, April 6). What having a "growth mindset" actually means. *Harvard Business Review*. https://hbr.org/2016/01/what-having-a-growth-mindset-actually-means?registration=success

29. Westaway, K. (2021, April 29). *Summary of effortless by Greg McKeown*. Forbes. https://www.forbes.com/sites/kylewestaway/2021/04/29/summary-of-effortless-by-greg-mckeown/?sh=27455dcc22e6

30. Intelligent Change. (2023). What is growth mindset and how to achieve it. *Intelligent Change*. https://www.intelligentchange.com/blogs/read/what-is-growth-mindset-and-how-to-achieve-it

31. Dweck, C. (2023, April 6). What having a "growth mindset" actually means. *Harvard Business Review*. https://hbr.org/2016/01/what-having-a-growth-mindset-actually-means?registration=success

DISCLAIMER

The information contained in this book and its components is meant to serve as a comprehensive collection of strategies that the author of this book has done research about. Summaries, strategies, tips and tricks are only recommendations by the author, and reading this book will not guarantee that one's results will exactly mirror the author's results.

The author of this book has made all reasonable efforts to provide current and accurate information for the readers of this book. The author and their associates will not be held liable for any unintentional errors or omissions that may be found.

The material in the book may include information by third parties. Third party materials are comprised of opinions expressed by their owners. As such, the author of this book does not assume responsibility or liability for any third party material or opinions.

The publication of third party material does not constitute the author's guarantee of any information, products, services, or opinions contained within third party material. Use of third party material does not guarantee that your results will mirror our results. Publication of such third party material is simply a recommendation and expression of the author's own opinion of that material.

Whether because of the progression of the Internet, or the unforeseen changes in company policy and editorial submission guidelines, what is stated as fact at the time of this writing may become outdated or inapplicable later.